The Bullies' Predatory Footprint

TERRI RYAN

The International Development & Information Guides

The Bullies' Predatory Footprint
©2013 Terri Ryan
ISBN No: 978-09523249-42

E-mail: bulliesvictimsandbystanders@gmail.com
www.bulliesvictimsandbystanders.com

Dedication

To my Mother for the endearing sweet lady she was, my Father for his extraordinary love of life and my brother Chris whom I had the privilege to know.
To my children, Clodagh and Darragh, who are my greatest gifts. Always be strong, enjoy life, and above all embrace love within healthy relationships.

Acknowledgements

I would like to thank Dennis Caulfield, Edel Redmond, Liam Silke, and Catherine Dolan for their help. Thanks to Steve Martin, Justin O'Sullivan, and Jackie Duffy for their intelligence and common sense. To my buddies who gave me their ear, Bill McWilliams, Angela Conlon, Esther McCarthy, Jane and Niall Egan, Kevin Morgan, Jim Murphy, Christi Byrne, Pauline Richmond, Fiona Byrne Annette Gavin, Mary O'Riordan,, Michael Mulally, John Keane, Mary O'Brien, Debbie Walters, Con Gibney, Ray Collins, Alan Broderick, and Gerry Hughes. To Gaines Hill and Jenifer Toomey from Create Space. To Roxanne Hearte, Mary Walsh, Jo Groom, and Dave Holland for their input. To Christine Croke, Natasha and Nenagh O'Gara, Fionn and Shane Croke. I would like to thank Sheila Harty, Professor Margaret Hodgins, Professor Adrian Frazer, and Professor Margaret Barry. Padraig Murphy, Dr. Jeffery Cooke, Dr.. M. Moran, Evelyn Ryan, Mary Barlow and Caroline Brennan. Pauline Folan, Violet Gavin, Lauri Allen, David Williams, Sean Higgins, Marie O'Shaughnessy, and Pat Quigley. Finally, and most important, I would like especially to thank my wonderful children, Darragh and Clodagh, for their patience and support.

E-mail: bulliesvictimsandbystanders@gmail.com
www.bulliesvictimsandbystanders.com

Contents

Preface ⌒‿

The Bullies' Predatory Footprint investigates all aspects of bullying across countries, communities, occupations, and cyberspace to capture and explain the behaviour on many different levels. The book is designed for men, women, and children everywhere who are bullied at institutional and interpersonal levels and find that they are unprotected through legislation and unsupported through communities to defend themselves against the behaviour.

Cyberbullying has highlighted the lack of protection afforded to citizens under current legislation to defend against the behaviour. Cyberbullying has also highlighted the lack of legislation attached to communities that gain financially from people who avail of services or work in these environments but provide no legal duty of practical guardianship to protect them against vile and cruel behaviour.

The book is designed to give a clear understanding of the behaviour of bullying to parents, children, employees, trade union representatives, teachers, nurses, doctors, human resources, personnel, psychologists, legal representatives, councillors, and health care providers who may be victims of bullying behaviour, or who may be best placed to witness or deal with the behaviour and prescribe remedies and solutions.

A global synopsis of surveys and legislation across different countries, communities, and institutions is designed: to provide advocacy groups, employees, parents, trade union members, and citizens with the necessary information needed; to identify whether current legislation protects citizens and victims against unwanted and cruel conduct; to determine whether governments ensure that the dignity and respect afforded in the founding principles of most countries are transferred to citizens; and to determine if unions succeed in putting people before profits.

The book is designed to emphasise the lack of any international acknowledgement, definition or regulation of the behaviour, and highlight the absence of any recording systems in place to quantify or monitor the extent of the problem.

The book is designed to provide a readable guide to libraries, third-level institutes, human resource managers, and schools by providing a broad research base into the specialist area of psychosocial risk behaviour. It is hoped the book will provide a practical support base on which to build awareness and training, and help to advocate more regulation in the area.

Through the web and e-mail address provided the author hopes that readers will be encouraged to tell their stories, communicate through an anti-bullying community, and re-visit the problem in a few years to see if changes have been made.

.

Introduction ❧

Millions of workers, elderly people, schoolchildren, and citizens are put at risk every day as the patterns of negative psychosocial behaviour become a phenomenon, affecting all countries, people, classes, and professions on a global scale.

Masterminding weaknesses, bullies transcend political, legal, and social boundaries, finding autonomy to exercise illicit, extraneous, provocative, cruel, and intimidating behaviour on others. In schools, workplaces, institutes, old-age care units, TV programmes, public offices, and social media sites, an explosion of the behaviour is experienced. Adjustments and controls needed to discourage and stem the behaviour have lagged far behind. The practice becomes incorporated into the value system, as authorities struggle to find the starting point, take a position, or agree—a definition. Children and adults, defenceless to stand up to the behaviour, choose to escape from its horrific effects through death rather than suffer further consequences.

Repeated tragedies produce an outcry from parents, teachers, trade unions, and political parties that draw the attention of the international media. The damaging consequences of the behaviour briefly emerges as a priority, which becomes reduced to nothing more than a humanitarian reflex when legal, economic, and social solutions are not followed up and sustained by legitimate action. As loss after loss is counted, the clarion cry from communities is heard from families and friends touched and disabled by its impact. A growing awareness is created in the minds of the public that this is not merely an episodic, individual problem but a broader issue rooted in wider social, economic, and cultural factors. Like sharks safe in the dark fathoms of the sea to prey on targets—decades of omissions to monitor, regulate, or financially quantify the cost of the behaviour has facilitated the behaviour becoming invisible, safe, and untouchable. These failures have safeguarded communities becoming the licensed grounds where contemptible and covert behaviour thrives, and cyber-serpents attack with venomous bile.

The culture of "might is right" and the exercise of dominance and power is legitimised on many levels in society. Violent movies and sadistic games proffer appeal to children as young as four, who become vicarious participants of violent action. The Corruption Perceptions Index (CPI)[1] keeps annual scores of illicit transactions breached by public officials in positions of trust who exploit their dominance and power for personal gain. Across the world, globalisation speeds up, and competition for transnational corporations and capital investment intensifies. Countries from diverse religious, cultural, and economic backgrounds are pitted against each other in a struggle to achieve economically driven goals, where cost competitions become a contemptible struggle based on the downward spiral of value owed to individuals.

Religious and political ideologies, lost in direction, traduce reason when nothing is done, and contradictions at the heart of moral and democratic values become evident. The value system is challenged, and existing rules are set in opposition as power and humanity are challenged to blend and unite. To date, no European or international definition of bullying behaviour exists. This has created conjecture, confusion, and delays to finding solutions, as definition provides the reference point from which statutes and standards follow. No requirement to report or record incidents of bullying has resulted in statistics being unavailable to support a need for legislative changes or make comparisons on a global context possible. Legislative initiatives to deal with the behaviour are almost exclusively confined to the workplace, yet negative psychosocial behaviour is reported in all communities. Institutions, companies, schools, workplaces, Internet sites, and elderly care units operate without any benchmark, convention, or recognised standard of care to determine if practical guardianship is provided or when unacceptable levels operate. Financial losses from violence and stress in the workplace, officially estimated in 2001 as being up to 3.5 percent of GDP,[2] have not been officially updated or extended to determine the total costs from other communities. These collective omissions have allowed negative psychosocial behaviour to be confined on a systems level to relative secrecy where tragedies alone become the catalysts for change.

The right of children to be protected from the behaviour of bullying has not been committed to the United Nations convention on the rights of children even in the communal areas of schools. No UN convention on the rights of the elderly to be free from bullying exists. Unwanted conduct on grounds relating to the sex, racial or ethnic origin, religion or belief, disability, age or sexual orientation is outlawed. In many countries this anomaly has led to further division and distinction, when no legislation has been extended to outlaw or protect unwanted conduct that violates the dignity of *all* children and *all* adults on *all* grounds.

Decisions to condone or outlaw hostile behaviour in many cases remain rooted in the political, economic, and cultural sensitivities of individual countries and communities. National ideals committed to cherishing citizens are weakened, leading to the simple critique that countries become too small, flawed, and ill-equipped to deal with problems that transcend international boundaries. This lends cogency to the fact that local solutions fail to tackle runaway changes, highlighting the need for countries to pull back, unite, and co-operate to find unilateral solutions to combat a culture of behaviour that is in danger of becoming a threat on a global scale. Authorities, failing to collectively associate, regulate, and respond at political or institutional levels, signal humanity at the crossroads. In an extraordinary perversion of *self-protection and fear*, communities can develop patterns of behaviour that indicate a paradigm shift in human empathy, as the phenomenon of collectively withdrawing into positions of silence spreads across the globe. Following the path of least resistance until it becomes the automatic route of human response, the natural instinctive inclination to help others—even in emergency situations—is suppressed. The collective cruelty known as the "bystander effect," or Genovese syndrome,[3] is unwittingly born, and the descent of negative psychosocial behaviour into savagery is silently witnessed.

The old cautionary tale once told in *Lord of the Flies* [4] starts to become the twenty-first century global reality, which in literal English translation means—Beelzebub.

Chapter 1 ∽
The Global Explosion of Bullies, Victims, and Bystanders

According to the Oxford English Dictionary, a bully is defined as a "person who uses strength or influence to harm or intimidate those who are weaker."[1]

The exercise of strength over weakness to intimidate or cause harm to others operates on all levels in society Dominance exercised by countries over less powerful nations is called jingoism. At an institutional level, citizens trapped within systems whose practices are oppressive and exploitative become harmed and choked by the institutional noose of excesses, corruption, and crony capitalism that is exercised. On an interpersonal level, the dysfunctional and harmful relationship between bullies and victims is established on the basis that the role of the victim is defined by repeated acts of dominance and cruelty chiseled out by the bully. The behaviour of bullying conflicts with the fundamental rights of people. It reduces human value, hurts human rights, and often ruins lives.

Most people have probably witnessed or experienced the behaviour of bullying at some point in their lives. Perhaps a family member was ostracized and branded the "black sheep." Maybe it was the dominant-and-submissive dynamic between spouses or neighbourhood gangs who "picked on" others just to watch their fear and pain grow. The escalation and prevalence of the behaviour over the past two decades, however, has created widespread concern across most countries and communities internationally. Wake-up call after wake-up call on the six o'clock news announces nursing homes forced to close because of elder abuse. The number of teenage suicides in the aftermath of school and cyberbullying increase, and landmark cases of libel and harassment are reported with accelerating frequency.

Like a game of consequences, these multifaceted forms of mistreatment are reminders that ethical, moral, and human connectedness is being weakened, and each event demonstrates that respect and human value is being eroded. New pastimes, such as "cruelty for fun" on the Internet, known as "trolling," and contemptuous fun practised during initiation ceremonies, called "hazing," are extreme examples of a wave of new behaviour. Nonetheless, this behaviour indicates a paradigm shift away from the way people interact and treat one another. Finding solutions has created a groundswell of discontent among people who feel they have become the disempowered majority. Pushed further and further away from positions of any influence, they observe their children, parents, and friends being mistreated, and are left with the overwhelming feeling of being powerless to change it.

To need acceptance and respect is in the nature of children. In contrast to the child, however, adult belonging is never as natural and playful and often has to be chosen, renewed, and regulated. Mother Teresa, who devoted her life to assuaging the suffering of the poor, said "being unwanted, unloved, uncared for, forgotten by everybody, I think that is a much greater hunger, a much greater poverty than the person who has nothing to eat." In the developed world, where hunger may not be a problem, a large number of people are bullied, undervalued, and unwanted. Unlike poverty, however, the ravaging effects of bullying on the lives of individuals and their families are not as outwardly apparent. No official system of monitoring exists to qualify or quantify the problem statistically or financially, which prohibits announcements being made on official platforms or public appeals being launched, calling for an end to the behaviour.

In France and Canada, bullying is described as "*le harcèlement, psychologique,*" which means an attack on the integrity and psyche of the individual. The behaviour encompasses a wide range of malicious and aggressive behaviour, including humiliation, mockery, threats, ostracism, and rumors. Targets that are persistently exposed to the behaviour can suffer from depression, stress, and anxiety.[2] Victims of bullying have frequently been diagnosed with post-traumatic stress disorder (PTSD)[3] and in many cases, show significantly higher levels of stress than patients suffering PTSD as a result of traumatic physical accidents.[4] Emphasising the seriousness of the problem, a Norwegian study conducted on victims concluded that as many as 40 percent of the most frequently bullied victims admitted to having contemplated suicide at some stage.[5]

Bullies do not come out unscathed either. Bullies were found to use drugs and alcohol, gamble, smoke, and engage in delinquent behaviour, with a significant tendency to hit their wives or cohabitees.[6]

Definitions of Bullying

The word bullying is used loosely across different countries and settings and is commonly interchanged with words, such as victimisation, mobbing, harassment, and negative psychosocial behaviour. In addition to the interchange of words to describe the behaviour, a multitude of names associated with where the behaviour takes place have emerged. These include "bullying in the workplace," "bullying in the schools," "cyberbullying," "corporate bullying," and many more. Although the same behaviour is experienced in all communities, each place is accompanied with its own definition, studies, surveys, reports, policies, and procedures. A fragmented, rather than a focused approach to finding solutions has resulted, which has inhibited the transfer of policies and legislation from one community to the other. Procedures found to be successful in reducing the risk of bullying in the workplace do not transfer to schools. Protocols in place to check for child abuse or neglect in state-run institutions does not transfer to the elderly, who suffer similar abuse and neglect in state and private-run residential care facilities.

Although many definitions of bullying overlap and concur, others remain unique to their individual country and culture. Definitions can range from a person's dignity being assaulted to a physical blow being delivered. Some experts confine the definition to repeated negative acts, while others see certain isolated incidents as constituting the behaviour. The word *mobbing* is specifically used to mean bullying in some countries, while in most others the term refers to collective gang bullying. The word *harassment* is commonly interchanged with the word bullying in language and in legislation to mean the same behaviour. Under EU Directives, however, harassment is defined specifically as when "unwanted conduct related to the sex of a person, racial or ethnic origin, religion or belief, disability, age, or sexual orientation takes place with the purpose or effect of violating the dignity of a person and creating an intimidating, hostile, degrading, humiliating, or offensive environment."[7]

The widespread confusion created through the use of terminology, and the overwhelming lack of unilateral agreement on definition have created huge challenges to conducting objective surveys, and has made any comparative studies between countries or occupations difficult. Conjecture and confusion on definition has impeded the introduction of legislation, as definition generally forms—the reference point from which statutes and standards follow. In practical terms, lack of definition has led to one person's account of being bullied being contradicted by another, when references can be selected from a multiplicity of definitions in use.

Popular definitions make the point that the behaviour is repeated and persistent, which over time has a cumulative negative emotional, psychological, and physiological effect. Many experts also concur that a power differential is achieved between the parties, with the bully exercising power over the target. Norwegian psychologist Dan Olweus, a pioneer of research into bullying, defines bulling as when "a person is exposed, repeatedly and over time, to negative actions on the part of one or more persons, when he or she has difficulty defending him or herself."[8] Pepler and Craig defined bullying as "negative actions, which may be physical or verbal, have hostile intent, are repeated over time, and involve a power differential."[9] The British criminologist Farrington defined bullying as being "repeated oppression, psychological or physical, of a less powerful person by a more powerful one."[10]

The Global Explosion of Bullies, Victims, and Bystanders
As trade and investment are intensified across the globe, the cosmos contracts to become one unilateral marketplace. An army of official supports, regulation, protection, and monitoring is used to ensure that the giants of trade and finance integrate and harmonise. No parallel measure of protection, support, or regulation is in place to ensure the unilateral human integration of

people. The gates of commerce are flung open to buyers and sellers who flood in to participate in cosmic combats of commerce where winners and losers are determined by market forces. People from religious, ethnic, cultural, and economic difference are pitted together in cost competitions with striking variations in the rules that determine how behaviour is conducted. Competitions without rules for behaviour are described in Latin as *canis canem edit*, which means "dog eat dog." As weak and strong line up to participate in the cut-throat competitions of commerce, they are quickly expedited in the global battles worth billions to define their positions as bullies, victims, or bystanders.

Bullies

The over-riding characteristic of a bully is the need to achieve success through dominance and control. There would seem to be no single path that leads a person to bully others, and the behaviour does not define the person or result in the denigration of that person as a whole. Bullies emerge at all ages and come from a diverse range of economic, social, and genetic backgrounds. The profile is far from simple, and bullies today can range from young corporate females to middle-aged male public officials with an age profile in children reduced to as young as five. The actions and behaviour of bullies have evolved to become more devious and ruthless than ever before. The behaviour is becoming the new psychological means to control, coerce, and get ahead. It is the new power tool used to exploit individual opportunities, gain influence over others, drive a financial deal, advance personal status, and achieve autonomy to illicit personal gain. Bullying can be used to exercise cruelty on others and breach positions of trust to achieve personal, emotional, psychological, or financial advantage, and will confront anyone who stands in the way of that ambition.

The compelling need to achieve what you want through dominance and control has many explanations. Reasons attributed to the perpetrator's behaviour include compensating for weaknesses and having poor social adjustment skills.

Competitiveness, jealousy, greed, resentment, rivalry, self-image, and a need to achieve have also been identified as motives. Studies and research have attributed some underlying causes of bullying to hormonal, neurological, psychological, and genetic factors. Some bullies have been described as arrogant and narcissistic, while others have been found to conceal shame and anxiety. From a young age, bullies may take a psychological advantage over others to compensate for a lack of skills, academic ability, or status. If this is found to be advantageous, it may be used as a continuum in later life as a means of achieving advantage over others. Bullies who have been bullied at home can believe from a young age that this is the normal way to behave. Bullies may "act out" to prove their authority and put others down in order to give the appearance of being tough. It may be that the accepted world of words, language, and behaviour acted out in video games may have created a "cool to be cruel" culture. Role models taken from TV programmes are all too often popularised as being the meanest mouth getting all the laughs. Mirroring this behaviour, boundaries in the boardroom and the classrooms are pushed to the next level — to get "a rush" from being mean. A reasonable link has been established showing that exposure to excessive and inappropriate television at an early age does have an impact on the development of subsequent bullying behaviour.[11]

Like all behaviour, it is suggested that bullying has its origins in childhood. Children who get their way through the use of manipulation, coercion, and dominance from the time they are very young quickly learn the power of these skills. When this behaviour goes unchallenged and unchecked, children learn that negative rather than positive behaviour gets them what they want. As the child matures, the behaviour develops and becomes more sophisticated. It adapts to become covert, camouflaged, and less obvious within the public, supervised structures of schools, third-level institutions, and workplaces. Throwing a tantrum as a child to get what you want might be substituted in later life for character assassination and humiliating others publicly. Although both types of behaviour are entirely different in expression, they are equally forceful forms of domination and control. These explanations may underlie some of the reasons why people bully and why the behaviour is escalating.

Victims

Anyone can be the target of bullying, and the bully has no particular exclusive prey. Gentle attributes, such as sensitivity and popularity, which may be perceived by others as talents, strengths, and beauty, can be interpreted by a bully as a weakness that they can exploit. How people internalise the abuse seems to ultimately determine whether a target becomes a victim to the abuse or not. Being removed from the emotional supports and reality checks that help protect against abuse can push targets into a weakened position and make them more vulnerable. Perpetrators describe some people as "easier to disarm and get at," leading to the belief that some people are more susceptible, vulnerable, and disposed to becoming victims than others. Targets with a "trusting" nature get completely caught off guard when people are cruel and mean. For some, being called an abusive name can have resonance from early childhood experiences. When similar abusive name calling is repeated in public, the linguistic assault becomes the equivalent of bullets from a machine gun. This can lead to an exaggerated response from targets and expose a weakness that makes them more susceptible to further attacks.

People who are different can be the most obvious choice for bullies to target. However, the focus of a bully's attention can be brought on by a target's gifts and abilities, as easily as their shortcomings. For many victims, the problems of bullying may be minor or transitory, requiring only support or intervention to get them back on the right track. Children who suffer deep emotional scars from being bullied can become profoundly hurt and find it difficult to overcome the experience. A common symptom reported by victims of bullying is bitterness. Grudges can develop and grow into a simmering hatred that later becomes expressed in horrific acts of revenge. In the aftermath of several high-profile shootings in schools in the Unites States, one of the conclusions made in the secret service safe school initiative report was that the "experience of bullying appeared to play a major role in motivating the attack at school."[12] A study by Pepler and Craig points to the fact that, in about 5 to 10 percent of experiences of bullying and victimisation, the problem became serious and required prolonged and comprehensive intervention to support adaptive development into positive pathways.[13]

Bully-Victims

The interchange between the role of bully and victim is not always what it seems. Executives who are the victims of workplace bullying can become petty tyrants in their own home, and bossy executives rush home at six o'clock terrified of being late for dinner. Bully-victims may start as victims and cope by becoming aggressors. Victim-playing can also be a fabrication used by bullies to continue a pattern of abuse. It can be an effective weapon disguised as a shield to divert attention away from abusive acts. It can be used to solicit sympathy or create leverage to manipulate a situation further. When bullies are finally found out, they commonly respond by crying as a coping strategy to gain leniency or escape harsh judgment by peers and colleagues. This is often followed by a list of reasons justifying their actions and a performance that could earn them an Oscar in the lead role as victim. Playing the victim can also be used to get attention, feed a victim complex, or seek revenge.

Bystanders

People who witness the behaviour of bullying but remain silent and passive are known as *bystanders*. Like the tip of a hat or a nod or a wink, the silence of the bystanders is seen by the bully as approval or permission to continue. Bullies rely on the general unwillingness of bystanders to speak up in order to maintain their position of dominance. Most groups will naturally form a pecking order or hierarchical model of command to some extent based on social, financial, or professional status. Bullies often become group leaders with top rank in the pecking order. In time, they can start to make an individual the "butt" of their jokes or highlight a target's lack of expertise or capability. If bullies face no objection, they continue to make inappropriate remarks and criticize targets. A regular stream of abuse and unwanted conduct directed at one individual becomes the accepted group experience. This behaviour can go on for months or years in offices, schools, Internet sites, clubs, and TV programmes.

In environments that lend themselves to a tolerance of bullying, bystanders often feel isolated, unsupported, and up against a culture they are left to challenge on their own. Within this culture, fear of being the next target and being rejected by the group is often what stops bystanders from speaking out. Fear of reprisals[14] and a lack of trust in management or teachers to handle complaints have led to millions of bystanders being silenced. Through their silence and passivity, bystanders play a significant role in becoming the unwitting collaborators and cohorts on the side of the bully. Like a fulcrum that provides a point to direct force, the silence of the bystander plays a central role in supporting the bully to apply dominance. Without an environment to actively discourage the behaviour, the silent support of colleagues, schoolmates, associates, and friends, together with weak laws, allow bullies to maintain dominance and control over targets. It is often the support of the bystander, or the illusion of that support, which causes targets to feel betrayed and finally defeated. When incidences of bullying are not addressed and few penalties are applied to perpetrators, the message is given that very little value is placed on how people are treated. Without support from legislation, advocacy, and trained professionals, a culture is created that accepts bullying as part of the value system. Unsupported and unprotected bystanders become afraid to step up, and silently step out.

The Dynamic of Bullying

The dynamic and characteristics of bullying, which set it apart from most other behaviour is that, a bully needs to be dominant over a target, and is in search of a subordinate who will surrender to that authority. A complicated panoply of manipulation, approval, charm, and brainwashing is used to seed and birth the dysfunctional relationship. Playing to the weakness of the target, bullies impose and reinforce their dominance in repeated acts that undermine the confidence of their targets. Placing on view every unsavoury fact or rumour about a target to make them feel fear, guilt, or inferiority. Targets are progressively led into an isolated zone, by a series of lesser choices they didn't notice they were taking, until they become eclipsed into the world of the bully. Increasing degrees of meaner and crueller acts are used to define the targets' inadequacy until they are overwhelmed by feelings of worthlessness and despair. Reversing their belief system, like a negative instead of a print, targets are slowly strangled by the continual denouncement of their individual validity until their resistance is broken, and finally respond in a way that is perceived by both as a—sign of submission.

Emotionally, Psychologically, and Socially Hijacked

Like an electric circuit complete when a switch is turned on, a signal of submission establishes a power differential that allows the emotional and psychological abuse from the bully to be directed at the target. Yielding to the will and authority of the stronger force, the target becomes— emotionally, psychologically, and socially hijacked. Submission will mean different things for different people. The legitimacy of one's strong or weak inner core, the patterns of behaviour repeated down through generations, as well as religious and cultural beliefs will all play a part in testing the point of submission. A sign of submission may not directly follow from acts of psychosocial violence but may be indicated in gratitude shown for the smallest leniencies, such as a smile when an occasional indulgence is given.

Trapped in their own disintegration, victims experience a range of disturbing emotions, such as guilt, inadequacy, vulnerability, embarrassment, anger, frustration, irritability, and a desire to retaliate. This is accompanied by fear, anxiety, difficulty in concentration, and disturbed sleep. Unprotected and powerless to change the dynamic, the target's daily torment becomes the repeated humiliation experienced in front of friends, family, peers or colleagues, and the dread of the behaviour escalating. Cumulatively, these emotions dull the targets' perspective, inhibiting their ability to initiate change or stand up to the bully. The range of incidents are widened and intensified almost in direct proportion to the targets' inability to defend themselves from the behaviour. What used to be solid ground beneath the victims feet turns to breaking ice, as the world they understood to be true shatters into confusion. Just as darkness is drawn to light until it is extinguished—dominance continues to be exercised until control is taken. Countries gripped in battles to claim sovereignty, would call this surrender or defeat.

Chapter 2 ∿

Pollution of the Psychosocial Environment

The psychosocial environment is an expression of the personality of a place. It is determined by attitudes, practices, design, values, and beliefs, which individually and collectively form the climate and culture of an environment. Psychosocial environments act to create an atmosphere as definite as a colour, influencing the way people interact, behave, perform, and participate. Practices that sustain and support toxic, hostile, negative values and beliefs encourage unhealthy interactive patterns of behaviour, which expose individuals to hostile environments that can eventually potentiate a risk factor to their mental and physical well-being.

Just as ecological environments become polluted by the dumping of toxic waste, attitudes and practices, such as bullying, fear, corruption, cruelty, stress, and hostility all create unhealthy psychosocial pollutants in communal environments where people gather to work, learn, retire, and play. For many decades this toxic behaviour has facilitated covert intangible and illusive forms of aggressive behaviour thriving. Cruel and sadistic behaviour, previously disguised in most communities, has been highlighted in recent years through the exposure of inflammatory messages and toxic posts in cyber communities. Exposing these acts of cruelty and the tragic outcomes that followed for many victims has brought evidence of the behaviour to the forefront of the public's attention for all the worst reasons. It has resulted in public outrage and calls for government intervention to introduce some regulation. The toxic behaviour experienced in cyber communities, however, is only a small representation of what is just the visible tip of many hugely contaminated communal psychosocial environments.

In all other communities, surveys alone indicate and alert the world to the existence of hostile negative psychosocial behaviour that children and adults must encounter daily. Surveys, commissioned periodically, provide scant insights and estimates that report the experiences of children in school as "a living hell," where they are in the "out-group," feeling insecure, unpopular, put-down, picked on, and excluded. Yet, these are the regulated environments where children are expected to learn, perform, concentrate, and achieve success. In the workplace, surveys document employees who work in hostile environments where they are subjected to physical and verbal abuse and degrading and humiliating conduct. Yet, employees must return daily to these environments to carve out livelihoods and maintain standards and productivity rates essential to national economic growth and success.

In 2011, the United Kingdom's trade union UNISON reported that six in ten workers were bullied or witnessed bullying in the previous six months.[1] In a study conducted in 2010 by the U.S. Workplace Bullying Institute (WBI), an estimated fifty-three million Americans reported they were bullied at work.[2] In 2007, 32 percent of school children aged between twelve and eighteen said they were bullied during the school year,[3] and up to 5.6 percent of elderly people reported being abused.[4] Survey after survey reports millions of people suffering from humiliating and threatening behaviour, physical assaults, verbal abuse, and harassment, which conjure up frightening images of hostile environments that tolerate negative behaviour as part of normal, day-to-day interaction and communication. As people wait for government authorities and unions to provide protection and support against this behaviour, its effects have started to be acknowledged as adversely affecting health—well beyond the usual counts of physical and psychological injuries we think of.

Child development books for parents are characterised by developing bonds and fostering respect and trust to nurture psychological, social, physiological, and emotional well-being. Starting school at age four, however, children can become exposed to rejection, name calling, false accusations, and rumours. Coming from loving families, children are often ill prepared for the abrupt and negative changes in their psychosocial environment. One minute, they are warm in the safety of the tribe in their home and are then plunged into a hostile school environment, where assumptions about their world can be broken down in the school yard in a matter of minutes, robbing many of their security, innocence, and confidence. In secondary schools, the environment can be even more dramatic and brutal. *Nobody left to Hate* by Elliot Aronson[5] was written in the wake of the Columbine High School shootings in 2000 to help teach compassion and make schools more humane by creating an atmosphere—"in which there is nobody left to hate." The severe detrimental effects of bullying in the workplace are also repeatedly emphasised. A study of a Swedish group of sixty-seven victims of bullying reported that among the most common symptoms they experienced were nervousness, insecurity, bitterness, self hatred, and suicidal thoughts.[6]

Children ready to start school and graduates taking up employment are often ill equipped to deal with the toxic and threatening environments they face. The question arises as to whether the duty of care in communal environments should be more clearly defined and regulated to ensure that they are more humane, or whether children and adults should learn the self-defence of bullying, to help protect against the behaviour.

Psychosocial Culture and Climate

Behaviour does not occur in a vacuum, and it is generally accepted that to some varying degree behaviour is influenced by the environment. Professor Lawrence Green, et al., a founding member of the Centre for Health Promotion Research and Development in Texas, argued that people cannot be treated in isolation from the social unit or system in which they operate or belong.[7] A basic ecological model of any social environment, as illustrated in figure 1, demonstrates that a range of factors in the environment influence and contribute to how people behave.

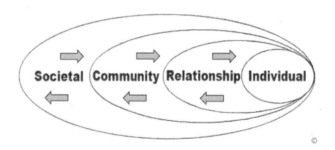

Figure 1. Basic Ecological Model of a Social Environment.[8]

An ecological approach to behaviour extends the emphasis beyond the individuals involved and includes the community environment as having a shared responsibility. Studies on bullying emphasise the need for investigations into bullying to include the interaction of the participants and the necessity to contextualise the environment, in order to help develop keys to unlocking barriers that prevent a reduction in interpersonal and organisational problems.[9] Including the environment helps to illuminate the behaviour comprehensively and give some perspective to the role that the environment plays in the development of unhealthy interactions. In practice, however, formulating anti-bullying policies and using intervention to resolve cases of bullying generally exclude the environment, and each case is treated as if no previous incident occurred.

Intervention involves investigating the behaviour between the individual parties, usually with concluding reports making recommendations for one of the parties to be transferred and, unfortunately, the target is usually the one asked to move.[10]

Focusing exclusively on the parties involved, however, deflects from investigating the culture and climate of the environment itself. Excluding the environment as a contributor to how behaviour is conducted facilitates inexperienced, lazy, and latent management practices continuing and perpetuates the continuance of inadequate policies and controls to regulate aggressive behaviour. It overlooks poor performance, inadequate guardianship, and organisational skills on the part of management and the operation of inefficient and out-dated equipment. It perpetuates the acceptance of attitudes and culture, such as discrimination and stereotyping, and collectively it facilitates and enables a tolerance of bullying and mobbing behaviour to survive and prosper. Failing to consider the environment smothers the possibility of bringing about any deep seeded fundamental changes in belief and value systems, which form part of the culture and climate of all psychosocial environments.

However, the responsibility of environments, such as institutions, companies, crèches, the Internet, schools, workplaces, or elderly care units, to play an active preventative role in managing negative psychosocial behaviour, has not been legally defined in most countries. The interpersonal dynamic of bullying behaviour remains confined to the parties and is dealt with as though the behaviour occurred in a vacuum.

In the workplace, studies have shown that the "principle determinants of workplace bullying have less to do with the characteristics of the victim, and more to do with the nature and organisation of the workplace."[11] In a study from the European Agency for Safety and Health at Work in 2000, ten stressors in the environment were found to act as antecedents to violence, harassment, and bullying. These were identified as including task design, workload, work-pace content, and work schedule. Other stressors included the organisational culture and function, career development, role in the organisation, work equipment, home-work interface, decision latitude, individual control, and interpersonal relationships at work.[12] These and other studies from school environments have helped to measure the capacity of the environment to impact positively or negatively on the behaviour of individuals. Few solutions can be found if stressors, which are identified by experts as being a primary cause of supporting repeated negative behaviour, remain rooted in the environment. These studies emphasise the need to define the environment in its responsibility to encourage or discourage inappropriate behaviour. The studies also highlight the role of the environment as a third-party participant that determines the outcome of positive or negative behaviour.

The Macro-Environment

The impact of the environment to influence behaviour extends beyond the immediate community into society where its influence is rooted in social, economic, and legislative practices. Aspirations to protect the respect and dignity owed to people in the macro-environment is underpinned and committed to the spirit, principles, and constitutions of international agencies and authorities, such as the United Nations, the International Trade Union Confederation, the World Health Organisation, the European Commission, the International Labour Organisation, Global Compact, and many others. Defining the respect and dignity implicitly owed to people at international levels ensures that overall aims to protect dignity and respect become acknowledged and defined at national domestic levels.

When no position is taken internationally to define the "duty of care" owed to citizens to be protected from hostile behaviour when in the care of third-party communities, overall aims become obscured, leading to piecemeal and fragmented solutions taken at national levels. To date, no agreement has been reached on any international definition of bullying. No convention, instrument, or directive has been introduced to define the legislative responsibility of any business, undertaking, or community to protect or provide a "duty of care" to people when in their care. Individually, protection against unwanted conduct that violates a person's dignity has been specifically prohibited in some countries on status-based grounds. In the United States, unwanted conduct directed at people, not protected under legislation, is referred to as "status blind" bullying. To date, the lack of collaboration at international and national levels to stamp out unwanted conduct on *all* grounds to *all* people has resulted in increased levels of negative psychosocial behaviour being experienced in all communities.

On a macro-economic level, unrestrained capitalism creates cosmic market forces that transfer to the national domestic economies of each country. The global "productivity squeeze" gets tighter and impacts on individual economies to become more competitive and productive. Employees spend more time working and commuting to work than ever before, becoming overstressed, overworked, unhealthy, and irritable. Financial stress transfers to "family and socially squeezed" relationships where human interaction is tuning out and going digital. The iPod, iPhone, iPad, TV, video games, and mobile phone are becoming the new operational connection with the world, suppressing human interaction and deadening human experiences. Children babysat with smart phones and amused with iPods, throw tantrums and become inconsolable when their toys are removed. Addiction centres now run digital detox programmes to help children as young as four to fight digital dependency and technology additions. Neuroscientists, such as Baroness Susan Greenfield from the United Kingdom have expressed concern about the negative impact of modern technology on children and called for studies into their impact on child development. Collectively, digital dependency reduces human permeation and intensifies individual insulation. It permits users to reduce their contact with people to the level of Information Technology or (IT) requirements, and treat people as an object or an (IT). Families and communities become socially splintered, and the basic, primal need to belong and be accepted in a group is torn away from where it was first nurtured. People with limited time and communities with limited funds experience a loss of social connectedness. Like trying to hold the tide back with a teaspoon, local activities and ideals of unification, which helped promote a culture of pride, respect, and co-operation, become weakened. Aloofness and insular activities are encouraged and a quest is sought for individual protection, self-fulfilling accomplishments, and solitary success. As the steady atomisation of the communal hub is lost, it is interchanged with self-ascribing individual needs, where commodities and possessions are substituted for belonging. In global markets that have transformed the landscape in which business is done, people compete in cut-throat financial warfare zones. Family relationships are squeezed and sacrificed in battles to achieve economic-driven goals. As international regulations focus and consolidate values, rules, and protections to secure continued global trade and financial integration, a human conflict arises when values, regulations, and standards that apply to individual human interaction remains undefined, unprotected, and unregulated in communal environments.

Indicators of Global Psychosocial Changes

Stock exchanges, the Dow Jones, and other indexes measure the landscape of financial markets 24/7. Physical elements of the environment, such as dust, bitumen, and noise, are measured and monitored and penalties apply if unacceptable limits are reached. Regulations apply to driving on public roads, managing litter, parking, and selling products and services. However, little or no regulation is in place to measure the way people are treated in communal environments. On January 16, 2013, Canada became the first country in the world to release a psychological health and safety standard. The Mental Health Commission (MHCC), together with the Bureau de Normalisation (BNQ) and the CSA group (CSA), released Canada's voluntary psychological health and safety standard, which is intended to provide employers in

Canada with a set of best practices to achieve measurable improvements for employees.[13]

The British Standards Institute (BSI) is also working toward a Publicly Available Standard (PAS) on the management of psychological risks. It is hoped the standard (PAS 1010 2011) will set a benchmark for psychosocial risk management, and increase and enhance awareness in this area.[14] The standard is seen as a route to promote best practice and a practical tool to help Occupational Health and Safety managers (OHS) successfully implement and maintain psychosocial risk management. Perhaps these standards will later be extended to award ratings to companies and institutions enabling workers to identify "healthy" organisations and affording parents a mechanism to identify "healthy" schools to send their children.

Stress— A Psychosocial Pollutant

Stress is a generic term widely used to describe people's negative reactions to pressures that they face when demands and expectations exceed their needs, abilities, skills, and coping strategies. *Distress* is the term used to describe the response of individuals to extended periods of stress, which studies suggest act as an antecedent to violence.[15] In 2007, a report published by the European Foundation identified stress as the second most common work-related problem in the EU[16] According to the 2007 annual report from the European Agency for Safety and Health, 22 percent of workers from twenty-seven member states believed their health is at risk because of work-related stress.[17]

Bullying— A Psychosocial Pollutant

The behaviour of bullying entraps victims and bystanders in a toxic dynamic that impairs self-confidence, impacts negatively on quality of life, and inhibits the ability to be productive and perform. In schools, daily doses of rejection, exclusion, and taunting pollute the environment of learning. It poisons the capacity to put moral and ethical teaching into practice, and reduces the capacity of schools to influence responsible citizenship. In the workplace, bullying behaviour was found to result in increased levels of absenteeism, estimated in one study to increase by 11 percent.[18] Bullying was also estimated to account for a 7 percent drop in productivity.[19] In public office, dominant behaviour can lead to autonomy that facilitates illicit acts of corruption. Psychologically, bullying results in nervousness, bitterness, self-hatred, and suicidal ideation.[20] Cognitively, it results in concentration difficulties, and emotionally it causes sleep problems, anxiety, and, in severe cases, victims are frequently diagnosed as suffering from post-traumatic stress disorder (PTSD).[21] A Spanish study published in 2002 concluded that about 16 percent of cardiovascular diseases in men and 22 percent among women corresponded to work-related stress.[22] As the cumulative mental, physical, and financial losses are added up, it becomes apparent that a fraction of the cost could be invested in preventing and reducing these problems if a commitment was made to the belief that people are worth it.

Scapegoated, Gaslighting and Cover-Ups

Gaslighting is a form of abuse often used in the aftermath of bullying to disorient victims. It is a form of psychological abuse in which false information is presented to victims with the intent of making them question their own perception of events and doubt their own memory. It is a tactic used to cover-up incidents of abuse in an effort to avoid financial claims or protect individuals. Gaslighting is designed to confuse victims and make them believe that they misunderstood the rules or imagined the behaviour. Skewed accounts of the incidents are often presented to victims, trivializing the behaviour or denying the incidents occurred. With no facts or witnesses to contradict the distorted version of events, victims may have to accept the wholly inaccurate characterization of their experience. Victims are not a consideration and they are effectively *scapegoated* to ensure the behaviour does not result in a claim or reflect badly on the profession or the establishment.

Instead of support and acknowledgement, victims can be accused of playing an equal role or told that they instigated or imagined the behaviour or misunderstood the intent of the bully. In the absence of legislation or an accepted definition of the behaviour or any official requirement to report and log the incidences, attempts at covering up and gaslighting are made easy. Victims of bullying who become victims of gaslighting have their experience of abuse compounded and prolonged, which can lead to long-term emotional, psychological, and physiological damage.

Corruption—A Systemic Pollutant

Corruption in public office is measured through the Corruption Perception Index (CPI),[23] which is the single largest cause of maintaining people in a state of poverty and misery. Corruption has left millions of citizens exploited and cheated, by having to pay back funds that were embezzled. It has resulted in tax cuts and cutbacks, which has sent people to *debt row* for generations, impairing and inhibiting their ability to live happy and healthy lives. Facilitated by ineffective anti-bullying policies, unscrupulous individuals have gained unrestrained access and autonomy to commit acts of corruption when in positions of power.

The Global Warning of Genovese Syndrome

Legislation and culture, together with social, legal, and economic policy, shape and determine the value system. Authorities, observing the mistreatment of others while doing little to change it, silently withdraw to adopt positions as bystanders. The phenomenon grows, and the communal response of individuals to the needs of others—even in emergency situations—is suppressed and replaced by a collective chilling and silent withdrawal. The bystander effect or the *Genovese syndrome* [24] sweeps across the globe in a type of frozen detachment that signifies a behavioural climate change—eventually placing people at risk in their own psychosocial environments.

Mobbing and Tornados

Mobbing is a particularly vicious type of gang behaviour where permission to conduct acts of repeated violence on a defenceless person is based on the twisted sense of reality that it's OK because "everyone else is doing it." The behaviour is typical of communal environments that are unregulated and toxic. The behaviour builds up a palpable velocity called the white tornado, causing destruction to everything in its path. Order fades and negative psychosocial behaviour escalates into a collective tribal, faceless, and reckless behaviour, where even the most outrageous behaviour takes on a semblance of acceptability. The cruelty directed at people who become defenceless to stand up to this behaviour has shocked communities, parents, and children worldwide. An estimated 10 to 15 percent of suicides in Sweden result in this type of bullying annually.[25]

The Predatory Footprint of Bullies

As negative psychosocial behaviour becomes uglier, the predatory traits of bullies escalate, and communities start to estimate the darker and financially costly effects of the carnage.

Like sharks safe in the dark fathoms of the sea to use their sensory lateral systems to seek out fish in distress, omissions and failures by authorities have resulted in safe environments being provided for bullies. The effect on victims, such as PTSD, burnout, suicide ideation, chronic fatigue, musculoskeletal and cardiovascular disease, are all indicators of a regression in human interaction and a medicalisation of what is a symptom of hostile psychosocial environments.

Lack of statistics to monitor the behaviour, an absence of financial evaluation to determine the cost of the problem, and little or no legislation to prevent or penalise its occurrence, has facilitated the practice of bullying going off-the-official-radar. In the absence of any safeguards to protect against the behaviour, the predatory skills of bullying become legitimately used to exploit the weaknesses of targets for financial, emotional, social, and psychological gain, and sometimes these skills of cruelty are exercised—just for fun.

Chapter 3 ⌒⌣
The Self-Defence of Bullying

In a relationship between two people, friendship, emotion, and labour may not necessarily divide evenly into positions of equal halves. However, the relationship between bullies and victims is established on the basis that the role of the victim is defined by the bully through acts of dominance and control.

Pepler and Craig defined bullying as "negative actions, which may be physical or verbal, have hostile intent, are repeated over time, and involve a power differential."[1] In a relationship between bullies and victims, polarised differentials of dominance and submission are established. When a person is completely subservient to a dominating influence, the subservient party is defined, according to the *Merriam-Webster Dictionary,* as a slave.[2] Within communities where no integrated approach is taken to creating a climate of safety and respect, a culture of negative psychosocial behaviour can easily be established, exposing targets to hostile attacks from bullies. Civil and criminal sanctions, suspensions, and disciplinary measures in schools and workplaces can follow from a physical assault, but in many cases no practical, legislative, or integrated support may be in place to protect targets against a psychological or emotional attack. Within communities where there is an expectation of trust and a belief that one should feel safe, being afforded no protection against a psychosocial attack can have devastating consequences. According to comprehensive studies, now conducted, the impact from more covert forms of violence, such as bullying, can, in many instances, equal the emotional trauma that follows from a physical assault.[3] Self-defence classes to protect against a physical assault are readily available, however, targets must often rely on their own supports and intelligence to defend their emotional and psychological integrity.

Awareness

To safeguard against a negative psychosocial attack, targets must first be aware of how bullies behave. Bullies are drawn to targets that can satisfy their need to control and exercise a claim over them. Targets are usually not aware of the need people have to be dominant or the destructive effect control can have. Awareness tends to sensitise targets to potential danger, by introducing objectivity that can stop short potentially dysfunctional connections before they even start. Bullies don't have any distinguishing features or characteristics to alert targets to the fact that they might be in danger. Unaware and unsuspecting of how bullies behave, some targets are more open to charm and manipulation, which bullies use in a duplicitous intoxicating cocktail that dulls the targets senses to their intent. A lethal mix of trust and authority, toughness and leniency, friendly and false is used to sneak up on a target. Targets that have a trusting nature and are unaware of the dynamic can find they are suddenly overwhelmed by feelings of fear, intimidation, and disbelief. They are unable to acknowledge what is happening, stand up to the bully, or seek help. To be acutely aware when a person is attempting to bully you is a great advantage and a powerful gift to give a person at any age, but most especially a child. Defensive skills to protect against unwanted behaviour can later be applied to situations in all aspects of life where hostile behaviour is experienced.

Isolation

Isolation is one of the hallmarks of bullying, and little by little bullies home-in on targets they single out as fair game. Bullies sense out targets by intercepting and exploiting signals that indicate distress or vulnerability. Targets with strong emotional supports tend to provide the necessary protection that act as a deterrent to bullies. Bullies see friends, family, and anti-bullying policies as a threat to their control. Targets that are isolated and cut-off from the common herd with no central support systems can attract the predatory characteristics of bullies. Isolating a target from their support systems is usually the first step in the process of dominance, which allows targets to be more easily brainwashed and controlled.

Words that Wound

Bullies are on the lookout for weaknesses or trigger points that have a resonance for targets, which they can exploit. Bullying behaviour usually starts with words, which are used to undermine a target and hook them into a position of weakness in the same way a drug dealer uses drugs to hit on a target until they are hooked as helpless addicts. Never underestimate the toxicity of the tongue and the capacity of words to be used as powerful weapons to strike pain and misery. A host of nasty comments, jibes, and remarks are used to exploit the weakness of the target and pry open emotional wounds to expose insecurities. A constant stream of negative words delivered in tones with more than just a hint of menace can force targets into feeling distressed and stunned. Nobody is perfect, however, people who feel insecure are more inclined to be more verbally wounded than those who acknowledge and take ownership of what they see as their shortcomings.

Hurtful and humiliating words delivered in front of friends, colleagues, or peers, can bait targets into the trap of retaliating back. Overwhelmed and hurt, targets can find it difficult to think straight and instinctively get angry. A reactive or over reactive response, given in the heat of the moment with knee-jerk speed, can be counter-productive. Exposing other people's emotional wounds and insecurities in public with the added impact of making them appear incoherent and inadequate makes the bully feel superior. It can also cause friends of the target to distance themselves, which, in turn, isolates targets further from their peer group, making them vulnerable to even more humiliating attacks.

While every bit as damaging as a physical blow, words and gestures can be accompanied by internal, critical self-talk, which usually proves destructive. Played over and over in the mind of the target, destructive words can inhibit quality of life, reduce self-esteem, and set a target up to become a looser in a contest or struggle with a bully.

Permitting the Bully to define Who you Are

Personalising what a bully says and taking on board the insult and shame intended makes a target much more likely to become quickly trapped as a victim in the dynamic of bullying. While abusive language says far more about the abuser than it does about the target, bullies have the ability to project thoughts and feelings onto the target. Bullies classically use repeated nasty inflammatory words, actions, snubs, and stares to reinforce negative projections onto a target. The bully has the ability to make these projections convincing and real and about the target. When the words and images projected by the bully are personalised by the target, the projections start to work. When the projections of the bully succeed in creating self doubt in the belief and value system of the target, the projections continue to work. When the projections of worthlessness and inferiority are believed by the target the bully starts to gain control, and the emotional hijacking has started.

Eleanor Roosevelt once said, "No one can make you feel inferior without your consent."[4] When targets personalise what a bully says—the target effectively permits the bully to define who they are. Permission does not mean it is given wittingly or willingly. Targets may believe a bully has knowledge of their deepest insecurity and become fearful of having this exposed publicly in full view of colleagues, friends, or peers. If targets have never discussed or shared their insecurity in a safe environment, permission to feel inferior can unwittingly and unconsciously be given by the target. The bully is not looking for imperfections but people with insecurities about their imperfections, so a reaction is drawn and they have permission to respond with further acts of aggression.

Eliminating the habit of translating what bullies say into personal terms eliminates the ability of bullies to exercise a threatening hold over a target. It also allows the target to be more objective. Victims who were bullied are often left with low self-esteem, feelings of inadequacy, and believing that they did not "fit in." Victims can often take years to reclaim their validity as individuals, restore their confidence, and reject the words of the bully. When the words are finally rejected, the experience has been described by victims as empowering and liberating. Victims finally start to believe that the nasty words and gestures directed at them were weapons of entrapment used by bullies to make the bully feel good and in control and had little to do with the victims personally. Having this knowledge beforehand can help targets deflect the projections of the bully and refuse the bully permission to define them as inferior.

The Social Context

Bullying is often referred to as psychological violence, but more accurately it is defined as psychosocial violence because of the social setting in which the abuse takes place. The social context is a characteristic that makes bullying behaviour uniquely cruel, as the target and the offender are linked together through a social group, such as an organisation, workplace, social site, club, school, or relationship. The "community" provides the bully with the opportunity to return, repeat, and reinforce the abuse, which adds to the impact of the contemptuous acts. The approval of colleagues, friends, family, or peers enhances the bullies' feelings of superiority and fuels the behaviour. Being repeatedly bullied within a communal group amplifies the experience of humiliation felt by the victim. It magnifies the feelings of inadequacy and rejection and quickly leads to a loss of standing, self-worth, and confidence. It goes to the core of the belief that one is "unwanted" and "does not belong."

Physiological Response

In addition to the psychological and social aspects of bullying behaviour, there are also physical and physiological aspects to the dynamic. Humans are designed to be on guard in case of being attacked, and the response of the brain to a threat or an attack has changed little over the centuries. When a person is bullied, a fear factor kicks in because the target feels under threat. Having wandered into an unfamiliar world, a threat sends a message to the brain, which causes the adrenal glands to secrete the chemical cortisol to help prepare the body to respond. Cortisol is pumped through the body, increasing heart rate and blood flow. Breathing speeds up, muscles tighten, and fists clinch. Whether you are being chased by a thief, humiliated publicly, or experiencing repeated unwelcome behaviour, the body feels under threat. The body cannot tell the difference between a threat that is perceived or one that is real and responds in the same way to the brain's call to arms by secreting cortisol, just in case. When targets are asked what is going on after an incident of bullying, they report pounding hearts, racing pulses, rapid shallow breathing, and shakiness.

Constantly weighing the implications of every incident and responding to threatening situations leads to anxiety, together with sleeplessness and physical weakness. Over time, the health consequences of coping translates into over secretion of cortisol and other hormones, which are pushed passed the upper limit, contributing to cardiovascular disease and exacerbates diabetes. As the behaviour continues, targets suffer a collective deterioration in their physical, psychological, social, and emotional ability to cope, eventually becoming unable and defenceless to stand up to the bully.

Detachment

Objectivity and awareness can help targets to see the bully as someone who feels good by making others feel inferior. Detachment helps targets to understand that the intent of the bully is to hijack their confidence. Targets can begin to understand that a reactive response sparks off the cycle and fuels the behaviour by drawing them further into the dynamic. This awareness helps targets to remain detached and objective about what is said. Through detachment, targets learn to take more control over the dynamic. They learn not to personalise what is said, which reduces and sometimes eliminates the negative projections of the bully. By staying detached and objective and not reacting or investing energy in a response, targets change the dynamic. It's like the dog won't chase you until you start to run. Don't run!

Coping silently is not detachment; this is suffering alone in silence. If targets try to numb their feelings against the fear they are experiencing, or try to find a way to become invisible to their abuser, they are not using detachment techniques. Detachment must be real and cannot be fake, put-on, or pretended. If victims fundamentally believe they have a reason to fear a bully, they will. The fear and worry felt will involuntarily trigger the bodies' alarm system. Trying to disguise fear and appear assertive or calm creates huge physical and mental stress on the body, which will become reflected in body language and the way they interact with others. Responding to threatened conflict by imposing controls to suppress the feelings of unease, is not detachment. Imposing controls will cause blood pressure to rise, muscles to tighten, and twitches to jump. Sleep is interrupted, and other psychosomatic manifestations start to surface. Being able to disguise a response of fear for brief periods to access rational understanding can be useful in the short term, but suffering in silence is a kind of avoidance that seldom works and is not an effective defence against bullying in the long term.

The Aftermath of Bullying

The self-defence of bullying succeeds when detachment is achieved. However, self-defence is not complete until the target understands that indirect appeals by the bully to feel guilt and remorse are invitations to start the cycle again. Targets can be told that the bully didn't mean what they said or that they were just having a bit of banter. Full of guilt and remorse, a target may start to believe the behaviour was all a terrible mistake. Guilt and remorse are private emotions internalised to regulate self-punishment and blame. Their proper management ensures that moral integrity and harmony are maintained and do not transfer to further personalising the wrongdoing. Targets should acknowledge an attempt was made to establish a position of dominance, which failed as a result of a good self-defence.

Suffering in Silence

Victims of bullying are often unprotected by legislation and unsupported by their community environments. Victims can often fear that by reporting incidents of bullying the behaviour will escalate further, and victims often remain silent. According to a study by John Hoover at the University of North Dakota at Grand Forks, 70 percent of children believed that teachers handle episodes of bullying "poorly."[5] In the workplace, employees are reluctant to report incidents because they are afraid of reprisals,[6] and elderly people fear that making a complaint will leave them more vulnerable to further abuse. Not having confidence in a supervisor, teacher, or health care provider to report incidents of bullying may be entirely justified. The fault may be due to a lack of investment in professional training and supports. Bullying can be a complex legal, social, and psychological problem that may need professional assessment, diagnosis, and referral. A lack of training, together with an absence of defined regulation and supportive anti-bullying procedures, has resulted in teachers, managers, and health care providers landing themselves in legal libel actions and undermining the confidence of many victims and bystanders to speak up. This has resulted in many incidents of bullying not being disclosed or reported, and, in many cases, it has made the situation worse rather than better, ultimately placing the safety of victims and bystanders at further risk.

Religious and cultural beliefs may encourage people to forgive the bully and turn the other cheek, which can be interpreted by the bully as permission to repeat further acts of abuse. Other people are taught to be assertive and confront the bully in the belief that the bully will instantly collapse, or reveal a true understanding of their deepest respect for others. While this may be very commendable, it is outside the scope of this publication and requires skill, confidence, experience, and ability. Those who asserted themselves against bullies in the past were often left doubting whether this convenient type of bully exists any more. Deciding not to confront a bully directly does not mean the behaviour is accepted. A target that decides to seek intervention from an informed third-party through the policies in place rejects the behaviour and calls for solutions to be found within the confines of the community where the behaviour occurred. Without a supportive third-party, a target is left on their own.

You cannot put plasters on an emotional wound, and degrees of professional counselling may be needed to restore the damage caused by negative psychosocial behaviour. Parents may need to explain the dynamic of bullying to children before they start school. Colleges may need to introduce modules to equip graduates with the necessary skills to prepare them to deal with the workplace environment. Third-level institutes may need to provide courses to equip professional with the necessary skills needed to use assessment, management, and intervention techniques to deal with the psychosocial risks that they may have to deal with in communal environments. Victims, who were fearful of bullies but felt they had to remain silent, explained their sinking feeling when they approached the school gates every morning. Like waiting to be taken down to the operating theatre, they described the feeling as one of despair and dread, where fear could do nothing but wait. Sneaking into school, shuffling in secluded corridors, they kept their eyes permanently fixed on the ground. Trying to stay safe from their silent assassins, the daily objective of targets became their need to stay as invisible as they could. Some victims said the feeling "never left them."

Chapter 4 ◦◦
School Bullying and Cyberbullying

As far back as 2000, the U.S. Secret Service reported that bullying was widespread and perhaps the most under-reported safety problem on American school campuses.[1] Since then, countless tragic incidents in schools have brought an increasing awareness to the fact that bullying has become a serious and insidious international problem within most school systems. As the realities of the same episodic tragic losses are counted, bullying takes on the dimensions of a plague that sweeps away the notion that children are cherished. The loss and outpouring of grief from parents, brothers, sisters, relatives, and friends strikes an uncomfortable cord that is often reduced to nothing more than a humanitarian response, when legal, economic, and social solutions are not followed up and sustained by legitimate action.

For children, the experience of school bullying is particularly cruel. Already struggling with adolescence, which brings its own changes and challenges, victims of bullying have their self-doubts and insecurities publically heightened. Hoping to find acceptance and belonging, children who experience humiliation and isolation from peer groups are made to feel unwanted and different from the rest. Parents whose children have been victims of school bullying describe the experience as a publicly humiliating persecution.

The transition from the environment of home to school can be more acute for some children than others, often leaving children from loving and caring families unable to cope with the concept of people being mean and nasty. Under the care of parents, children are protected against all risks to their health and safety under various legal guardianship acts. State intervention to remove children from the care of parents can result if they fail in their duty to protect their children. In the event, however, of a child being bullied in a state-run school, which presents a risk to the child's health, there is no requirement for the school to report the incident. Parents can be powerless to request intervention or ensure the school accepts any responsibility for failing to prevent the risk. The duty of practical guardianship by the school may depend on the aptitude and attitude of the local principal or teachers, and the quasi-operation of anti-bullying guidelines and codes of practice. While it is difficult to regulate behaviour that is scaled up to the level of school ratios, there is an expectation that schools should be more proactive in a defined legal duty to protect children from negative psychosocial behaviour.

The school environment is a microcosm of society wherein children develop physical, cognitive, social, moral, and ethical skills. In the school setting, research and studies have shown that bullying behaviour undermines the learning environment and presents an obstacle to the development of cognitive skills, such as concentration and performance. The emphasis in schools, however, is often directed solely on academic achievement, and the underground swell of negative psychosocial activity that finds its way into the lives of hundreds of children who gather together each day is ignored. The ethos of moral teaching is often lost to children who find it difficult to reconcile lessons taught on treating people respectfully with the experience of witnessing a tolerance of bullying in the school yard. Being a central tenet for teaching ethical behaviour, schools that fail to adopt models for treating people with respect is an opportunity missed, primarily for individuals and ultimately for society.

Perhaps more than any other school safety problem, bullying affects students' "well-being," and the ill-effects have been shown through empirical evidence to result in the development of a constellation of symptoms. A study on the effects of bullying among school children aged eleven, thirteen, and fifteen across twenty-eight countries was shown to cause headaches, sleeping difficulties, irritability, and bad temper.[2] In another study of students attending coeducational secondary school, the effects of somatic symptoms, social dysfunction, depression, and absences, were examined and found to be experienced by both boys and girls to varying degrees.[3] The attributed association in extreme cases of bullying behaviour with suicides[4] has been popularised by the use of the word *bullycide*, however, it should be noted that general studies on the subject of suicide show that a person rarely commits suicide for just one reason.[5] Those who bully were found to be more likely to use drugs and alcohol in later life and also engage in subsequent delinquent and criminal behaviour.[6] Despite the consequences suffered by many pupils, however, schools often support the practice of bullying by failures, omissions, silence, culture, and a lack of professional support and training for teachers.

Teachers, who are often best placed to witness and deal with cases of bullying, are not provided with any professional training on bullying intervention as part of their professional training qualifications. The requirement to manage negative psychosocial behaviour in schools does not form part of the teaching contract of employment. School grading systems rarely include a comparative category that refers to anti-bullying prevention policies and standards. In most countries, school anti-bullying policies are requested and recommended through government departments but are not mandatory. Problems associated with bullying are dealt with loosely under guidelines, checklists, insurance policies and the intervention of teachers. Serious breaches of conduct are dealt with through parental intervention and referrals to social services and the criminal juvenile or justice system. Disciplinary measures, sanctions, or penalties are not imposed on schools or school officials for failure to introduce or enforce anti-bullying policies.

School Bullying

Communal belonging and acceptance plays a significant role in the life of all teenagers, which is universally recognised as a rite of passage into adulthood. Through links with others in their school year, teams, and clubs, teenagers develop a sense of community and identity. Communal belonging becomes a source of great pride and joy, which builds confidence, friendships, and strength of character. When this camaraderie is misled or misused by people with an agenda against others, a group of teenagers can quickly turn tribal. School bullying tends to escalate beyond the individual parties involved, as others are encouraged to join in a collective type of gang bullying know as *mobbing*. Logic was never the focal point of any strongly held tribal identity and a gang of school children with raging hormones can act with great abandon when no central conscience is in place. Gang behaviour develops its own energy and momentum with its own rules, as members of the mob collude in the shared goal of abuse in exchange for belonging and acceptance. Ritualistic displays are acted out in public demonstrations of dominance and defiance. Systematic and repeated negative acts are directed at the target, which can quickly escalate out of control and climax in devastating and savage consequences for victims. Targets are bombarded with texts, emails, and posts on social media sites. The gang gathers in packs to intercept the target on the way to and from school, and after-school swoops are made around the target's home. The target is tripped, pushed against lockers, and taunted. The relentless acts of cruelty, rumours, and jibes become a twenty-four-seven ordeal from which the target gets no break. Monopolised by the constant reminders of inadequacy, worthlessness and not "fitting in," victims are cast into a world where they lose perspective. Inhibiting their ability to initiate change, targets are distracted from being able to find constructive help or stand up to the bullies. Friends of the target, afraid of being socially demoted to the "out gang" or becoming the next target, join in the mobbing behaviour. The ganging up of friends or team mates is often seen by the target as a final act of betrayal and defeat.

Investigations that followed in the aftermath of several tragic incidents of school bullying have shocked and horrified communities worldwide. The level of cruelty perpetrated by gangs of school children against solitary and vulnerable victims was described by some—as torture.

The Role of Schools

Preventing bullying in schools is not new. Studies by Pepler and Craig indicated that bullying and victimisation placed a child at risk of a range of problems in later adolescence and adulthood. Looking at bullying from a developmental perspective, they argued that the combined use of power and aggression found in school yard bullying underlies problems that continue throughout life. They noted that "children who learn how to acquire power through aggression on the playground may transfer these lessons to sexual harassment, date violence, gang attacks, marital abuse, child abuse, and elder abuse."[7] While many people continue to see bullying as part of the school experience, a continuum of the behaviour into all aspects of society creates a destructive social and financial drain on society. Interrupting patterns of behaviour through intervention and preventative strategies during the formative school years can, therefore, become a critical issue in eliminating or at least helping to curtail the problem. When no intervention takes place, the individual victims ultimately suffer the consequences, and society pays a huge price on multiple support systems and remedies.

As the primary developmental institutions of society, schools have a bigger onus than ever to counter the negative effects of bullying behaviour and to provide safe environments that support the acceptance and validation of all children. Intervention programmes have been adopted by many schools in a downstream investment to interrupt and influence the pattern of bullying behaviour in later life.

A "whole school" approach has been developed by many educational authorities in response to school bullying. This approach includes an integrated system that introduces anti-bullying procedures and the logging, reporting, and investigation into incidents of bullying. Training, discussions, and curricular activities are organised to counteract the perception that violent behaviour is an acceptable part of ethical and moral teaching. School activities are supervised and monitored. Support programmes are in place for victims affected by bullying, while restorative measures are used to influence a change in the behaviour of offenders. Working with local agencies to combat all forms of negative psychosocial behaviour is encouraged, as are in-service training days for parents and teachers. Codes of conduct are introduced, and checklists and evaluations are made by inspectors to determine whether programmes and policies are implemented and effective. School posters are made visible to reinforce anti-bullying messages, as are days dedicated to celebrating differences and uniqueness, which all forms part of a "cultural shift" away from what was traditionally taught in schools. The "whole school" approach is most associated with the pioneering work of Dan Olweus in Norway.[8] He developed the Olweus Bullying Prevention Programme, which has been operating in schools for over twenty years. The programme is built on four key principles, which are structured into the school social environment to address both the individual and organisational determinants of bullying. The programme operates in eighty schools in Norway and has been adopted by many other countries. The "whole school" approach was found to be more successful and effective in reducing levels of bullying in schools than traditional piecemeal approaches that dealt with problems on a crisis-management basis. Reactive responses were found to concentrate on the effect rather than the cause. In these cases, the opportunity to diffuse the behaviour was often lost, and the situation escalated and became externalised into the community environment.

In Australia, an approach called the Friendly Schools PLUS programme is also used to reduce bullying in school communities.[9] It draws on thirteen years of extensive research from the Child Health Promotion Research Centre (CHPRC) with an emphasis on building social skills. The Friedly Schools PLUS programme is recognised nationally and internationally as a whole-school evidence-based programme that can reduce bullying behaviour.

To curb violence among students, many schools have implemented conflict resolution programmes. These programmes tend to follow six key principles where the central focus is the constructive management of conflict.[10] The skills transfer to the classroom and can also be applied with confidence beyond the school to any situation that involves conflict. A restorative justice approach, also used in schools, contrasts with the traditional retributive justice approach of apportioning blame and seeks to combat bullying behaviour by reintegrating all parties back into the community.

The Role of Communities

Communal interaction in the home is not as apparent as it once was, and verbal discussion has become rare. Timeout is often time logged online, and playtime has commonly become cyber participation in violent games. Splatterhouse, Kindergarden Killer and a host of other video games promote violence as a form of recreation, where the aim of the game is human annihilation. Video violence has helped popularise the "cool to be cruel" culture, and the school yard often becomes the playground used to re-enact violent games, get a laugh, and become a real live hit and a hero. Reasonable associations have now been identified between excessive early television viewing and the subsequent development of bullying behaviour.[11]

In the past, schools have been seen as institutions separate from other local services and in charge of their own problems. The jurisdiction for school policy traditionally stopped at the school gates, but the continuation of the aggressive behaviour is more commonly externalized into the local community, where it can quickly accelerate into criminal or fatal outcomes. More than ever before behaviour in schools is being strongly influenced by the surrounding community, and partnerships are being encouraged to develop strong links to regulate hostile interchanges between both communities.

Families of children bullied in school can often take sides and quickly get caught up in a dynamic that develops into a private war. By taking the law into their own hands, families can lose sight of the main issues and develop into secondary feuds. Schools with joint initiatives and partnership links with the local community become key factors to finding solutions. Taking the wider community into consideration, attention focuses on objective intervention strategies in schools. This helps avoid intervention being interpreted by children and parents as taking sides, and helps ensure that stigmatisation is not attributed to school staff and pupils. Developing links between the community and the school also encourages cooperation from parents which can be used constructively in joint initiatives to reduce aggressive behaviour.

The Role of Police
Strategies to reduce the levels of school bullying and aggression have turned attention to the increasing need for schools to seek

inputs from community police and call on the intelligence and expertise of the criminal justice system. Without professional training, teachers who try to deal with incidents of bullying can often make things worse. Students, who report incidents of bullying in school, have been made targets on social media sites with posts calling them snitches, sneaks, and tell-tales. Graffiti smeared on community walls and toilets become a constant reminder to others not to speak up. This has led to wide ranging consequences for children and teachers, often culminating in a total breakdown of trust in the school reporting system. Without specialised training, teachers often prefer intervention that is objective, as they can feel compromised in their dual role of being asked to intervene in incidents of school bullying, especially when they live in the local community. Community police officers, already performing a liaison function to develop positive links with schools, are increasingly asked to participate in anti-bullying programmes. Inputs are given into conflict intervention courses, which can be learnt more easily in the controlled setting of the school and then applied to the less controlled setting of communities. Increased police security has also become a feature following from attacks on schools, which has led to the issuing of safe guides to prepare schools for unwanted intruders.

Monitoring Bullying in Schools

Incidents of school bullying are generally not recorded locally, and no official agency or central system is in place to monitor incidents nationally. Government agencies responsible for school policy do not have statistics available to allow trends and patterns to be analysed on an annual basis. Huge swells of negative psychosocial behaviour from the local community pour into schools with little or no guidance, support, expertise, or funding to acknowledge or address these new challenges. Left to their own resources and discretion, schools often fear that preventative measures will draw more attention to the behaviour and lead to litigation and a culture of compensation claims. Although prevention and early intervention are the most appropriate ways to deal with the problem, schools are often faced with the consequences of the behaviour after an incident occurs.

Statistics are a valuable source of information to monitor problems and help provide reliable data to influence the need to introduce changes in policies, legislation, or reform, especially in schools that are experiencing rapid changes in ethnic, religious, cultural, social, and economic diversity. Without statistics, predictions for future disasters and crises are reduced to guesswork. Crisis-prepared schools systematically collect and analyse early signs of distress and aggression, cultivating a sense of being prepared. Crisis-prone schools deny the possibility of a crisis happening, which increases the chances of severe disruption and harm occurring if a crisis does arise. Gathering statistics gives greater insights into reading any warning signs and allows time for incidents to be prevented, averted, or mitigated.

CCTV Monitoring

Away from the watchful eye of adults bullying often takes place in transition areas, where there is little or no supervision. These areas include hallways, locker rooms, stairs, restrooms, cafeterias, school buses, bus stops, and the main entrance to the school. More and more CCTV monitoring is being used by schools when they are left with limited resources for supervision. CTTV monitoring can act as a deterrent to covert forms of aggressive behaviour and also provides a reliable backup when conflicting accounts of bullying incidents arise and insurance claims are pursued.

The Self-Defence of School Bullying

At a time when establishing acceptance in a peer group is paramount to belonging, hormones are racing to make all kinds of unpredictable, unexpected, and unwanted emotional and physical changes. Teeth get braced, the skin is pimpled, and the voice cracks. Stature, size, and shape become constant challenges, along with bald and hairy dispositions and sexual changes. Jibes transfer to names, such as *gawky, geeky, dorky, flat-chest, busty, fatso, string-bean-skinny, knock-knees, frog-eyes, concord nose, and cauliflower-ears.* No teenager has the appearance of the robot perfect pin-up, and even the great beauties of the world did not escape from "teen taunts." A menu of "put downs" will serve to severely test most targets in the school environment more than any other environment they are likely to encounter in later life. Individual differences, however, are what make each person unique, real, and human. Embracing uniqueness defines who people are and shapes who they become. Accepting individuality defines people as winners or losers in their own contest or struggle in life. Individual uniqueness stays for life, and people who reject their uniqueness can become more vulnerable and open to attack from bullies. The struggle to accept "who you are" is a personal journey, and if allowed to be externalised into the school community can become a public personal persecution.

As with all bullying, retorts and rebukes are short-lived, and tit-for-tat matches usually end in combat. With an audience drawn from a peer group, the target and bully can become trapped in a game of painful words thrown in both directions. When tit-for-tat matches are conducted in the school yard or in public, a target can easily be baited into retaliating back, which usually makes matters worse. In what becomes a primal battle, both parties are challenged to end with a winner and loser, and the ultimate winner is often judged to be the dominant party, achieved through fair or foul means. Not participating in verbal tit-for-tat matches is a good strategy and a smart self-defence to surviving the school years. The old sticks-and-stones school rhyme was commonly used by pupils, parents, and teachers to offer comfort to children suffering from the verbal taunts and actions of bullies. When chanted over and over, it may have provided soothing comfort to help dull the pain, but it may have been cold comfort to others who never stopped believing the humiliating taunts and hurtful words said.

"Sticks and Stones may break my bones, but names will never hurt me."

Being prepared is a much better defence to bullying than being surprised by the behaviour in the school yard or chanting a soothing rhyme. An age-appropriate book for young children to become equipped to deal with the dynamic of bullying is called *Wicked Wiggly Words* by the author Terri Ryan.

The Extent of Bullying in Schools Internationally
In many countries, statistical information on school bullying remains scarce or absent with only sample surveys providing estimates of the problem. Results from surveys include:

Australia – A self-reported study published in 1999 estimated that one in six or seven children indicated that they were bullied on a weekly basis.[12]

Britain – In a report published in 1994, 4 to 10 percent of students were found to be bullied per year.[13]

Canada – In a 2000 report, 15 percent of children up to eighth grade said they were victims of bullying behaviour.[14]

Germany – Between 4 to 12 percent of students reported frequent and persistent bullying in a report published in 1999.[15]

Spain – A report found that 15 percent of secondary school children were bullies or victims of bullying behaviour in a report published in 1999.[16]

United States – A study found that 20 percent of fifteen year-old students said they had been bullied in the current term at school.[17].

A study of junior high and high school students found that 77 percent of students had been bullied in their school careers.[18]

Legislation

Multiple cases of deaths associated with school bullying have been reported around the world, yet legislation in most countries to prevent school bullying still remains absent. The UN Convention on the Rights of the Child (UNCRC) advocates in Article 19:1:

The "parties shall take all appropriate legislative, administrative, social, and educational measures to protect the child from all forms of physical or mental violence, injury or abuse, neglect or negligent treatment, maltreatment or exploitation, including sexual abuse, while in the care of parent(s), legal guardian(s) or any other person who have the care of the child."

Article 19.2 states: "Such protective measures should, as appropriate, include effective procedures for the establishment of social programmes to provide necessary support for the child."[19]

Article 19.1 of the UN convention for children refers to the term *mental violence,* which is reflective of a victim's state of mind. This term suggests that the onus may fall on victims to demonstrate deterioration in their mental health to prove that bullying took place, rather than let the evidence "speak for itself" and show that preventative measures were not in place. Incidents of bullying that fail to be resolved must be tested in public legal battles that pit parties against each other to produce evidence of behaviour within a system where the behaviour is not defined, and the role and duty of the environment is not defined or regulated. No specific legislation usually exists to address the problem, and no European or international instrument, convention, or directive acknowledges the problem exists. This would seem an unfair position to place a child who becomes a victim of bullying, when no legal requirement exists to exercise any practical duty of guardianship to prevent the behaviour.

The litmus test of legislation to protect children from unwanted conduct is provided by its ability to stop cyberbullying. In the past, children suffered outrageous acts of abuse through behaviour that could not be proven, in communities that could not be challenged, by children who did not have a voice. Cyberbullying, however, makes it evident that twisted and wrong behaviour can be conducted with devastating consequences for children. Cyberbullying also highlights the fact that communities remain legally untouchable through the current legislation that is in place to protect children.

Duty of Care of Schools and Insurance Obligations

Despite the constitutional rights of children to be protected, the "duty of care" of schools as guardians of children is often not legally defined. Guidelines and codes of conduct often form the basis for guardianship with no penalties or disciplinary measures attached for breaches or non-compliance. The parameters of managing bullying behaviour are often defined within the guidelines of insurance policies, which outline the safeguards needed to protect the school against potential litigious challenges. Counter legal challenges of defamation, together with children under the legal age of adulthood, present difficulties for school authorities that look to policy makers to strengthen children's rights. To avoid legal challenges, schools popularly advise parents to transfer their child, where responsibility for the child's safety is hoped to legally transfer back to the parents.

Cyberbullying

Cyberbullying is defined as the "wilful and repeated harm inflicted through the use of computers, cell phones, or electronic devices," which is often referred to as e-bullying. While all communities can provide havens for bullies, nowhere is the cruelty more visible than in the vile allegations, personal rumours, and hateful humiliating comments posted on social media and internet sites. In the absence of unilateral international legislation to regulate these negative acts of psychosocial behaviour, the international cyber community has become a global free-for-all. The instant messaging culture has become a worldwide web of people who spread hatred and misery and don't think or take stock before they post or send, often harrying vulnerable children to commit tragic acts of suicide.

Technology, with the capacity to bring people together, create links, and give people a voice, also allows personal information, and vile humiliating allegations to be made available to an audience of millions in nanoseconds. The lack of international legislation to hold community environments responsible for regulating behaviour is magnified in the fibre optic communities of cyberspace. Free from state guidelines, codes of conduct and adult supervision, social media sites become self regulated and provide a state-of-the-art sophisticated means of cruelty that uses no forcible entry, leaves clues, but can't be touched. The teenage community, who are the largest users of YouTube, social media sites, and other techno trends, are targeted by "trolls" who sweep the net in search of cruelty for fun, and cyber-serpents that spew venomous bile with lethal repercussions for innocent victims. According to the Cyber Research Centre in America, about 20 percent of children aged eleven to eighteen become victims of cyberbullying. Their research found that mean or hurtful comments were reported by 13.7 percent of children, and the spread of rumours was reported by 12.9 percent of children.[20] According to their research, both boys and girls were likely to report feeling angry, sad, and embarrassed. A joint EU study in 2010 with the London School of Economics conducted in twenty-five European countries found that 6 percent of nine-to sixteen-year-olds had been sent nasty or hurtful messages through cyberbullying.[21] Cyberbullying geographically transcends the school gates, and some schools rely on this to avoid taking any responsibility for dealing with cyberbullying. Other schools take the view that they will deal with cyberbullying if the behaviour is shown to have an impact within the school setting. This attitude may appear regretful, but, in many cases, schools are given the responsibility of dealing with cyberbullying without guidance, support, expertise, or finance.

Offences under legislation regulating landline phone services relate to messages sent that are grossly offensive, indecent, obscene, menacing, or known to be false for the purpose of causing annoyance or needless anxiety. This legislation also applies to communications made through mobile phones and other electronic communication. A fine or term of imprisonment is imposed if a person is convicted of any of the offences listed under this legislation. The legal adult age for bringing a prosecution against an individual, however, varies within individual countries.

Reporting inappropriate mobile phone usage must be initiated by the victim in a signed statement to the police. Permission must also be given to the service provider to allow the identity of the caller be made without infringing data protection laws. Other options to stop cyberbullying may exist under criminal legislation, such as stalking, which refers to offences committed when a person is persistently followed, watched, or pestered by any means. An offence is also committed under discrimination and equality legislation, if unwanted conduct is directed in a discriminatory manner through any means of communication.

One of the major difficulties with social media sites and emails is that people tend to treat them informally, and a person's integrity and reputation can be assaulted and impugned quite casually and publically. Things are said in electronic communication that would not be said if talking to a radio presenter or a news reporter. However, the same laws of defamation and libel apply to defaming a person by letter, email, newspapers, posts, or through cyber message boards. Civil cases against invasion of privacy, breaches of data protection regulations, and defamation and libel as a result of electronic communication have been successful. However, social media communities have welcomed the veil of anonymity through the use of pseudonyms, which makes perpetrators more difficult to identify.

Individuals taking legal action against social media moguls could be a logistic and legislative challenge, presenting a minefield of jargon in transnational jurisdictions. Defining the duty of care to protect citizens within the public cyber community has now become the battleground of techno giants and governments.

Tragedies in Schools

School shootings with scenes of death and injury occurred in Thurston High School in Oregon, United States; Dawson College in Westmount, Canada; Dunblane Primary School in Scotland; Neuilly-sur-Seine in Paris, France; Columbine High School in Colorado, United States; and Sandy Hook Elementary School in Connecticut, United States. These shootings have stunned and horrified the world, leading to extensive analysis, debate, and investigations. In a number of cases of school attacks, it was found that the attackers had experienced bullying and harassment that was long standing and severe and was described in terms that suggested the experiences approached torment. In one case, most of the attacker's schoolmates described the attacker as the "kid everyone teased." In witness statements, schoolmates alleged that "nearly every child in the school had at some point thrown the attacker against a locker, tripped him in the hall, and held his head under water in the pool, or thrown things at him."[22] Other school tragedies shocked the world, such as the death of fifteen-year-old

Phoebe Prince, who was bullied in school in Massachusetts and committed suicide in January 2010. This tragedy led to the introduction of the anti-bullying bill, which was passed by the Massachusetts Senate on March 9, 2010. This legislation was followed by New Jersey enforcing the toughest anti-bullying laws in U.S. schools on January 5, 2011.[23]

Signs of Bullying

Signs of bullying can be easily missed, especially with teenagers and parents who have a lot going on. Some signs to look for:

- Deteriorating homework, loss of interest in school, and an inability to concentrate
- Loss of confidence, appetite, and increased irritability
- Poor attendance, arriving late, and taking long routes to and from school; asking to be dropped far away from the school gate
- Being withdrawn and showing a reluctance to go out
- Obvious upset after reading texts and checking social network sites
- Shortage of money
- Torn or dirty clothes, missing or damaged possessions
- Repeated signs of bruising and injuries
- Requests to drop out or change schools
- Recurring headache and tummy pains
- Distressed reactions, such as stammering, nightmares, and bed-wetting

Anti-bullying policies and healthy school environments become an increasingly important issue for parents. Catastrophic events have created mistrust in the minds of many about the capacity of the educational system to protect children's safety. It has also created lingering doubts about the capacity of the educational system to create healthy environments that enhance the ability of children to concentrate and learn. It draws attention to the growing belief that there is a need to look at school reform, which may well be overdue.

Chapter 5 ∕∾

The Predatory Playgrounds of Workplaces

It is difficult to believe that in the well-established, regulated, workplaces of the world incidents of bullying behaviour are still tolerated. After all, the collective economic strength of most countries depends on their smooth operation. Unions represent workers to ensure their rights are upheld, safety committees deal with health and safety issues, and statutes of labour and employment laws apply. Human resource functions manage and resolve day-to-day personnel difficulties. Vast amounts of money are spent reaching standards of excellence and quality marks. State services are freely available and accessible to employees and employers to resolve any disputes that arise. The terms and conditions of work are set out in the employment contract and in return employers have a "duty of care to employees." It would be reasonable to presume that the duty of care of the employer would include protection from threatening behaviour, verbal abuse, humiliation, bullying, harassment, and physical assaults.

However, a worldwide survey of workers, conducted in May 2011 by the Monster Global Poll found that 83 percent of European respondents reported they had been physically or emotionally bullied during their careers. In the Americas the figure was 65 percent, and in Asia 55 percent of employees reported being physically or emotionally bullied.[1] The European Foundation listed work-related stress as the second most common work-related health issue across the European Union, (EU) in a report published in 2007.[2]

Despite the alarming increase in the number of bullying incidents appearing as a workplace hazard, however, stress-related illnesses are not listed on the EU schedule of occupational diseases,[3] or the International Labour Organisation (ILO) official list of occupational diseases.[4] Falling outside the official list of occupational diseases, no statutory obligation exists to notify stress-related illnesses to occupational health and safety authorities. Bullying behaviour, which acts as an antecedent to stress,[5] goes off-the-official-radar for detecting any risks to the health and safety of employees. These omissions have resulted in no assessments, or hazard auditing procedures being required to regulate or reduce the risks caused by negative psychosocial behaviour to employees. This situation has collectively facilitated unscrupulous individuals being protected in the practice of bullying in the workplace for decades.

The workplace is not just where people come to earn their livelihood; it also provides opportunities to achieve enormous financial success and status. Loaded with degrees of authority and financial remuneration, the workplace creates formalised power differentials that invite people to exercise the trappings of power and dominance over others. Financial rewards can be created or destroyed, and careers can take off or be cut short. With so much to gain or loose, unregulated workplaces can become the predatory playgrounds where psychopaths and dysfunctional bullies thrive.

Exalted status attached to titles like superior, supervisor, senior, director, principal, and boss quickly lead to the establishment of power differentials of importance, entitlement, and superiority over lesser beings, such as assistants, juniors, public servants, and subordinates. These titles all imply a subservient role to a higher power that must be obeyed. In addition to titles, other power differentials are established based on grade, rank, and increment, which often reflect authority related to time served rather than any measure of responsibility, achievement, or expertise held. Hierarchical organisational structures can also facilitate bullying behaviour, by placing frontline staff into positions where they are overwhelmed by work overloads and suffer stress, verbal abuse, and harassment from customers, clients, and patients for the latent mistakes and inadequate practices of senior management. Surveys report bullying behaviour in huge numbers across most workplace occupations, and increasing numbers of civil actions from discrimination, dismissal, libel, and sexual harassment in the workplace are reported through the media.

The largest proportion of peoples' lives is spent at work with years of education spent achieving costly qualifications beforehand. When employment is finally secured, a person can innocently walk into a bully-ridden work culture and experience the impact of negative workplace behaviour as a shocking and personally devastating experience. Teachers and nurses, attracted to caring professions, can find they are working in occupations where the incidents of bullying are amongst the highest in the world. Creating an awareness of unacceptable behaviour during the induction period is as significant as a first impression. It sets the tone and establishes the parameters for the type of behaviour and communication that is expected. The opportunity to create the first impression and establish ground rules, however, is often lost by employers who fail to provide training during the induction period or at any stage of employment. New employees often find they are up against an accepted culture of bullying they never anticipated and are unable to challenge. Tactics, such as character assassination, ridicule, gossiping, exclusion, and humiliation, become a standard practice. When no anti-bullying preventative measures are in place, employees become particularly vulnerable and defenceless to stand up to the behaviour.

Relationship difficulties in the workplace can go hand-in-hand with most occupations where employees and managers are confronted on a daily basis with work-related problems. Diminished resources, cutbacks, and problematic budgets can all lead to frayed tempers and personality clashes. However, if a line is not drawn between a "dust-up" and the behaviour of bullying, a problem slowly develops. Associates and friends become the unwitting observers of the ritualistic bullying behaviour targeted at colleagues. In an escalating process that can start with just a stare or a word, the behaviour progresses quickly. Inadequate training and key information is withheld, leading to unfair criticism and work targets set up to fail. Public humiliation brings its own condemnation, leading to swift and decisive assertions by colleagues that the targets' standing has become impaired. Awkwardness, professional distancing, and isolation from other employees become the norm.

Returning day after day to experience the same repetitive feelings of degradation can have a cumulative psychological, physiological, and emotional impact. The professional integrity of the target starts to be called repeatedly and unmistakably into question by colleagues and supervisors. Promotions, career, and income become threatened, and sick leave, depression, insomnia, anxiety, absenteeism, and addictions often follow. Victims may eventually feel forced to reduce their hours or leave their employment, which can often be the strategically well-planned outcome orchestrated by the bully.

Men traditionally bully directly, especially if they are in senior positions, but they also attach themselves to gangs. According to a study conducted in 2010 by the Workplace Bullying Institute (WBI), 62 percent of bullies are men and 38 percent of bullies are women.[6] Women typically "pair bully," which involves one and maybe two others. The female bully is active, while the passive cohorts who observe and support her are known as her "bitches." Another finding of the WBI study was that women bullies target women in 80 percent of cases, and men target men in 44 percent of cases.[7] Gang or group bullying occurs when other colleagues gang up on a co-worker. This type of behaviour is particularly covert, profound, damaging, intangible, and difficult to prove. Typical negative acts would be gossiping in groups with the exclusion of the target. Sending emails to "the gang" with the exclusion of the target is the norm. This sends a message to the target that he or she is being talked about. The email is selected to trigger a strong reaction, which causes shock or laughter and generates discussion from which the target is excluded. Group activities are organised with the omission of the target, which is further compounded when the event becomes the widely discussed topic of conversation the following day at work. Group giggling, whispering, or sneering after an individual target makes a casual comment is also common. This behaviour indicates an underlying code understood only by the gang that the target is "left out of the loop." The gang decides when the air conditioning is regulated, when the heating goes on and off, and when windows are opened or closed. Although affected by these actions, targets are not included in the decision making.

Protected through mutual support and acceptance, group behaviour can escalate. Individually, people may be aware the behaviour is wrong but in the absence of training awareness and weak management, nobody has to confront this inconvenient truth. The behaviour intensifies, and rumours circulate about the target that extends beyond the immediate work environment. The victim may also become the scapegoat for inefficiency and random acts of wrongful work practices, including theft. As it becomes increasingly difficult for the victim to retaliate, the experience becomes overwhelming. Making a complaint can be counter-productive, resulting in fuelling the behaviour further, when plausible justifications given by the bullies collectively outweigh the victim's account.

Definition of Workplace Bullying

No internationally accepted definition of workplace bullying exists; neither is there any agreement of what constitutes the workplace. Different terms are used by different countries to describe the behaviour, which include *bullying, victimisation, moral harassment, psychological violence, mobbing, employee abuse, covert aggression, intimidation, negative workplace behaviour, and hostile or negative psychosocial behaviour.* A menu of definitions can be selected from various authors, specialists, and academics across the globe. The definition adopted by the ILO is "any action, incident or behaviour that departs from reasonable conduct in which a person is assaulted, threatened, harmed, injured in the course of, or as a direct result of, his or her work."[8] The definition goes on to make the distinction that internal workplace violence is "that which takes place between workers, including managers and supervisors." External workplace violence is "that which takes place between workers (and managers and supervisors) and any other person present in the workplace." It has also been defined by an expert advisory group as "repeated inappropriate behaviour, direct or indirect, whether verbal, physical or otherwise, conducted by one or more persons against another or others, at the place of work and/or in the course of employment, which could reasonably be regarded as undermining the individual's right to dignity at work."[9]

The Role of the Workplace

The distinction between the interpersonal dynamic of bullying between individual employees in the workplace and the bullying that results from the characteristics of the workplace itself are not often dealt with. To address this lacuna they are dealt with separately here.

Popular definitions of workplace bullying generally exclude the workplace environment and confine the behaviour to the interpersonal dynamic that takes place between the individual parties involved. Negative psychosocial behaviour in the workplace, has therefore become dominated by impressions and images of "disgruntled employees" and "unhappy and angry" people who come to work and interact in a manner that triggers bullying behaviour. Attributing bullying behaviour solely to the individuals involved, has led to anti-bullying policies focusing exclusively on the behaviour of the target and the bully.

Academic research and study, however, has found that many of the triggers to negative behaviour in the workplace are complicit with management practices and culture. Empirical and qualitative studies have found that "the principal determinants of workplace bullying have less to do with the characteristics of the victim, and more to do with the nature and organisation of the workplace."[10] These findings are important, not least because they suggest that "if the principal drivers of bullying are organisational in nature, then appropriate workplace practices and policies can be developed to reduce, if not eliminate the problems."[11] These studies emphasise the capacity of workplaces to diffuse or trigger employees being exposed to bullying behaviour and suggests a defined role of responsibility must be assigned to the workplace. At an organisational level, the financial and management context in which prevention and intervention of bullying behaviour is mitigated and improved often rests exclusively with the workplace. The workplace itself, therefore, forms the basis for how negative psychosocial behaviour is managed. No amount of interviewing and intervention between employees will fix a build up of tension that is caused by unfair and over demanding workloads or remove negative attitudes, such as discrimination or stereotyping that is accepted at management level. Mainstream books and training courses for management, contain no reference to any responsibility, expertise, or function required to introduce management practices and technology to prevent or reduce potential conflict between employees

Failing to identify the environment as the third-party participant contributing to the outcome of positive or negative psychosocial behaviour supports the workplace as having no defined "duty of care." Sweden, Belgium, the Netherlands, and France now acknowledge the role played by the workplace to conduct well-managed work practices in order to reduce workplace violence. Environmental and labour legislation in Norway and Denmark places obligations and responsibilities on employers to prevent and reduce the risk of violence in the workplace. Placing responsibility on the environment has been achieved by introducing a hierarchy of organisational risk-reduction techniques.

At an organisational level, the use of designs, fittings, furniture, surveillance, and access restrictions are adopted as a first-step approach to counteracting bullying behaviour by using Crime Prevention Through Environmental Design (CPTED) techniques.[12] Although traditionally applied to the retail and health care sectors to reduce physical violence and crime, the CPTED approach is often integrated into interior design, layout, lighting, car parks, and toilets to reduce the risk of conflict. A commitment from the highest level of management to support anti-bullying is also seen as an essential step in the process of reducing bullying behaviour as well as a commitment to introducing policies and training modules to raise awareness of unacceptable negative psychosocial behaviour. This approach is further complimented by the introduction of risk assessment techniques into situations where conflict may arise in the workplace.

Reduction and preventative measures are used, which require risk assessments and specialist management practices to identify potential ticking time bombs that can be diffused by applying management analyses and conflict resolution techniques. Management must first proactively identify the determinants of bullying behaviour, anticipate the negative outcomes associated with these determinants and design procedures and strategies to review, refine, and counter this behaviour. Audits are undertaken regularly to establish the risks of negative psychosocial behaviour to employees in line with standard health and safety practices that are applied to physical and chemical hazards.

Not applying risk assessment preventative techniques to negative psychosocial behaviour reduces organisational anti-bullying policies to little more than token gestures when risk factors that can contribute to negative behaviour are not addressed through health and safety risk assessment procedures.

Organisational Triggers to Bullying

Risk factors that lead to an escalation of bullying behaviour are unique to each work situation, but many factors have been identified as being common to most. Typical organisational triggers to bullying arise when large imbalances in gender, background, and personality differences exist. Work goals and sales targets that are solely performance-based with no accountability for the associated treatment of people were also shown to cause an escalation in negative psychosocial behaviour. Organisations where job opportunities and promotions were viewed as crony back-scratching rewards that operated to rig the system for the benefit of the few were found to lower staff morale and cause deep interpersonal resentment and hostility. Overcrowded, poorly ventilated, badly designed, dirty, and noisy premises were also found to experience higher rates of violence than those that were maintained in good condition and exhibited good physical design features.

Management practices, which included taking prolonged periods of time to make decisions, were identified as one of the principal causes of bullying behaviour amongst workers. Bad management practices resulted in slowing down performance and creating unjustified delays and queuing, which induced negative attitudes and aggressive behaviour. When organisational problems were persistent, they were found to cause powerful negative mental strain in working groups, where "the group's stress tolerance diminished, causing a scapegoat mentality that triggered acts of rejection against individual employees."[13] Poor interpersonal management skills that operated in "closed" authoritarian working environments where people worked in isolation and mutual suspicion also escalated the risk of violence, as opposed to "participatory" working environments, which helped diffuse the risk of violence.[14] Negative climates were also found to be driven by poor organisational skills that placed excessive workloads on specific individuals, while leaving others relatively inactive. Labyrinthine bureaucratic procedures also produced the same effect. Lack of role clarity to define workloads and duties and a lack of job training also led to confusion, disagreement, and negative behaviour. An escalation of bullying was also shown to coincide with organisational changes, such as a new manager or supervisor, a change in ownership, reorganisation of the company, or the introduction of new technology.[15]

Bullies become skilled at determining if anti-bullying policies can assist their behaviour rather than their victims. In the absence of smart policies, bullying can be used to exploit, coerce, and pick on one employee after another by preying on the vulnerability of others to achieve success. Employees aspiring to an ethos of respect, personal responsibility, and fair and open competition would be well advised to check anti-bullying policies before signing a contract of employment. In the United States, the tort of negligent hiring is recognised in twenty eight out of fifty states.[16] Employers can be held responsible and accountable for failing to screen applicants by checking their background and references before placing them into positions of high public contact.

When Bosses Are Bullies (Bossing)

The prime perpetrators of bullying in many surveys have been identified as bosses.[17] Hired into formal positions of authority to exercise control over others; bosses can operate with unquestioning dominance and control. Being bullied within this hierarchical relationship, employees are often afraid to report the incidents because of reprisals that might follow.[18] Employees may also believe a complaint will trigger an escalation in the behaviour and result in certain privileges being withheld. This situation can be further complicated by formal complaints procedures, which must be reported through the line manager, with no other secondary channels of reporting available.

Employees, afraid to make a complaint, become concerned about having benefits, such as overtime, holidays, break-time allocation, and family friendly policies, reduced, which are often decided at the discretion of the boss. They fear work performance may be vetted in a way that impacts negatively on their promotional prospects. They worry that work distribution or unattainable work targets will follow or that they will be physically isolated and given no work to do. The ultimate fear for victims making complaints against bosses is that their careers will be kicked to the curb or they will be victimised and baited into the trap of being found unable or unfit to do their job and effectively "bullied out."

In the event of a dispute between an employee and a boss, employer liability insurance often provides legal cover to owners and senior managers. Protecting senior staff, whether in private or public office, is seen as protecting the company or the establishment. In instances of bullying, where both parties are working for the same employer, taking one side above the other in advance of a third-party determination would seem unfair, especially in public or official office. A guarantee of paid legal representation to senior management, however, regardless of the behaviour, can effectively act to support and safeguard inappropriate behaviour at senior level.

Hierarchical relationships in the workplace are boss driven, and the success of the relationship is often what determines promotions and future job references. Through their responsibility and job description, managers exercise their "right" to get workers to execute work targets. While this does not include their "right" to bully, drawing a line between legitimate management practices and the behaviour of bullying and harassment can sometimes be difficult to determine. When anti-bullying policies do not address organisational triggers to bullying, this line is left to the discretion of the boss, which makes this line even harder to define. Ironside and Seifert claimed that a clash between a bully and a victim in the workplace becomes a collective issue, which is inherently and unavoidably inequitable "becoming enmeshed in the fabric of workers and managers rights."[19] As long as workers are economically dependent on their jobs, they can find themselves in a weakened position. In times of recession and economic down-turns, "putting up" with being bullied in exchange for a job can amount to a lifetime of clock watching and a type of aching incarceration that has started to define many careers. Employees that feel forced to leave their employment will say they "left their managers and not their jobs."

Vicarious Bullying
Vicarious bullying is quite common in workplaces where the bully is not directly involved in the behaviour but is the third-party who is instrumental in instigating the behaviour. The behaviour typically arises where a boss deliberately stokes conflict between employees, particularly in situations where a boss feels threatened

by an employee. Differences in professional, social, and financial status can often make superiors in rank, title, and grade feel envious, threatened, and undermined. This envy can lead to a subordinate's life being made difficult and can lead to them being made to appear incompetent. Without any direct contact with the parties, the boss is uniquely positioned to change workloads, disrupt training schedules, and arrange to have certain information withheld from one of the parties. By introducing impossible work targets, combining different personality types, and orchestrating a change in work demands, a boss can manipulate a situation to set one employee up against the other. Difficult and intangible working situations build up, followed by angry jibes, distrust, and resentment between colleagues, which can quickly escalate into negative behaviour and interpersonal conflict. As the boss observes the plot thickening, they wait for a complaint to land on their desk. The duplicity of the boss, acting to resolve the situation, while escalating the source of the trouble ensures that the target continues to suffer from the repeated acts of humiliation and hostility directed at them from colleagues.

Employees caught in a bully work-trap can find leaving their job difficult. They are dependent on the job to meet financial and family obligations, but find returning, each day, to the workplace to be a degrading, humiliating, and psychologically damaging experience. Ironside and Seifert argued that bullying was a basic part of the management of labour and "that most of its forms are accepted as part of the daily experience of employed work." They argued that "bullying is endemic in labour management practices associated with making a profit."[20]

The Aftermath of Bullying in the Workplace

Gaslighting is a form of psychological abuse in which false information is presented to victims and is commonly used as a tactic by management to deny incidents of bullying occurred. Built into the procedures for reporting incidents of bullying, management must first be informed of the incidents. Management facilitates the parties to resolve the incidents of bullying through intervention. This approach can, however, later be used by unscrupulous management to betray this position of trust by bombarding the victim with misinformation and repeatedly and collectively reinforcing the distorted view that the incidents did not occur. The incidents may be re-labeled as "operational matters" or as "a personality clash," which completely disorientates the victim, making them doubt their own memory and perception of the reality of what happened. In the absence of any recording procedure or witnesses, victims are left with nothing to reinforce their own view of the truth, except the account given by management. In an attempt to offset legal challenges, block a complaint, or reduce a personal injury compensation claim, the victim's experience of being bullied is prolonged. It compounds the behaviour of abuse and makes victims feel further humiliated, inadequate and betrayed, which can lead to far reaching consequences and long-term damage.

Resolving Complaints of Bullying in the Workplace

Across the globe, anti-bullying preventative strategies and expertise is substituting positions of authority and control with competence and ability. Its principles are rooted in values of enterprise, democracy, and fair play. Anti-bullying promotes practices that work to help ensure decisions are made for the benefit of the majority and not just the few. Anti-bullying policies ensure that latent and lazy management practices are weeded out and that technology, technique, and talent are promoted. Anti-bullying practices motivate employees to perform to the best of their ability rather than struggle with feelings of being humiliated and bullied. Although preventative measures and the reduction of organisational risk factors have proven to be the most cost effective strategy to resolving incidents of unwanted conduct, the most common solutions still continue to be an increase in management capacity to resolve disputes after they have erupted. Instead of anti-bullying policies forming part of the risk reduction function, which the prefix "*anti*" suggests, anti-bullying policies typically only kick–in after an incident of bullying occurs and a complaint is made. Following from a complaint, the parties are called to give an account of the complaint to a third-party. The parties are then facilitated to find a remedy. If this process does not resolve the situation, the matter may progress to the formal stage, which requires a written complaint to be made. This stage is followed by a formal investigation conducted internally or externally by a dedicated team, which usually includes employer, employee, and trade union representatives. Decisions taken exclusively by management to select and agree fees with a private investigator can compromise an investigation. Private investigations command expensive fees for investigators who may have no specific qualifications and no affiliation to a professional body in the event of an unfair investigation or bias shown towards either party. When the investigation is complete, a report is compiled, making a conclusion to uphold or turn down the complaint. The parties concerned may be the only people questioned, if no witnesses were present. If conflicting accounts are given, it becomes a question of who the investigator believes. If an employee goes out sick because of an illness, employers exercise the right to request a second medical opinion. Medical assessments are increasingly conducted by forensic psychiatrists to determine if the medical condition suffered by the victim has a causal link to the behaviour allegedly perpetrated by the bully.

Industrial Relations Procedures and Tribunals

Collective agreements between trade unions, employer groups, and government officials have resulted in the industrial relations mechanism being put in place to resolve workplace disputes. Disputes that cannot be resolved through the internal workplace procedures can be facilitated through the industrial relations mechanism, which operates under labour authorities, tribunals, or commissions. Through the industrial relations process, disputes are dealt with less formally than in the courts and usually include the option of third-party mediation. Matters that fall within the industrial relations framework usually have limited time frames to bring disputes and, with exception, are confined to six months from when the last incident occurred. To initiate a dispute, an application must be filed to the appropriate authority, setting out the nature of the complaint. The official website or authority will outline the list of acts under which disputes can be raised and the appropriate forms can be downloaded. Notice is then sent to the employer and both parties are notified of the date and venue for the scheduled hearing.

The industrial relations acts may not relate directly to the behaviour of bullying, but relief may be obtained through other remedies. A union official or solicitor can make representation on behalf of the applicant, or applicants can represent themselves. Written submissions are made to the tribunal, which are relied on at the hearing. The hearing is presided over by one or more officials who hear the case and make recommendations, which are later given in writing. The recommendations can be taken up by both parties or appealed to the next stage. If the industrial relations procedures do not succeed in resolving the dispute, the matter can be brought to the courts.

Resolving Issues through Legislation

Legal redress through the courts must also adhere to the statutes of limitation, which impose a set period of time to take an action. Depending on the nature of the dispute, remedies may be provided under a wide range of legislation that encompasses bullying behaviour. These include: constitutional law, harassment, health and safety, sexual harassment, equality, anti-discrimination, employment, environmental, labour, civil, common, human rights or criminal law. A breach of the contract of employment or a personal injury insurance claim may also be appropriate, which are dealt with in Chapter 9.

Monitoring Incidents of Bullying in the Workplace

As no official system of logging and recording incidents of bullying is in operation in the workplace in most countries, the national scream of a bullied workforce remains unheard. Psychosocial illnesses are not officially listed as "occupational," so no statutory requirement exists to notify or report these illnesses to the Health and Safety authorities, and no statistics are published in official annual summary Health and Safety reports. At best, national surveys, conducted periodically, provide estimates of the problem—which offer a very slow response to reporting behaviour that is escalating at an accelerated pace. Failure to gather statistics on illnesses that are a direct result of negative psychosocial behaviour ensures no attention is drawn to the problem. No statistical information is available to canvass trade unions, advocacy groups, or governments to introduce changes in legislation. These omissions and oversights ensure the behaviour continues.

The official requirements of national Health and Safety Authorities and the EU Directive 89/391 /EEC[21] require employers to record absenteeism as a result of "occupational illness" for more than three days. The current system does not require absences to be recorded that result from psychosocial behaviour. This omission makes quantifying the cost of absenteeism due to negative psychosocial behaviour only possible, through self-reporting surveys. Collectively, this distances employers from any financial responsibility or obligation to introduce preventative anti-bullying risk reduction procedures. The omission allows stress and violence to continue to strike at the health and well-being of workers. The omission allows the behaviour of bullying to continue to strike at the economic strength of industry, which was estimated as costing up to 3.5 percent of GDP [22] in 2001.

Chapter 6 ∾
Global Surveys on Bullying

Surveys provide an estimate rather than a statistical account of any particular situation or event where sample polls are taken from sections of the community and applied as typical of the community in general. In the workplace, pioneering surveys and research began as far back as 1980 in the Nordic countries. Initiatives to estimate the extent of bullying in workplaces across the rest of Europe largely began in the late Nineties. These initiatives were prompted, to an extent, by the introduction of the 1989 EU Directive 89/139/EEC, which was "to encourage improvements in the safety and health of workers at work."[1] In order to guide policy makers on the requirements needed to transpose the EU directive into national law, surveys were conducted across most member states. The reports that followed from these surveys were often the first account of workplace bullying in these countries and demonstrated a phenomenon of behaviour that affected millions of workers, transcending status, occupations, sex, age, and social origin. Following from these surveys, some trade union and employer groups began to conduct surveys on a regular basis. In most countries, however, no official substitute system for gathering statistics replaced the system of surveys or polls to estimate the extent of the problem. In this chapter, surveys in the workplace are addressed, and surveys conducted within communities, such as schools, are dealt with under these dedicated chapters separately.

The Extent of Bullying Internationally

Australia – The Australian Council of Trade Unions (ACTU), regularly conducts specific surveys on work-related stress and safety issues, which are made available on their website.[2] A comprehensive series of empirical studies conducted across Australia found: 50 percent of workers in third-level education experienced verbal abuse, 39 percent experienced threats, 1 percent physical assaults, and 65 percent experienced bullying. In the health-care sector: 67 percent of employees experienced verbal abuse, 33 percent threats, 12 percent assaults, and 10.5 percent bullying. With taxi drivers, 81 percent experienced verbal abuse, 17 percent threats, and 10 percent experienced assaults.[3]

Europe – A 2011 Monster Global Poll posed the question: "Have you ever been bullied at work?" The survey found European respondents experienced the highest incidence of bullying with 83 percent claiming to have been physically or emotionally bullied during their careers.[4]

Germany – In 2010, the German *Deutsche Welle* newspaper reported that labour experts and psychologists estimated that 1.0 to 1.5 million workers per day were victims of bullying.[5]

Ireland – A national survey of bullying in Ireland in 2000, reported that 23 percent of respondents in the workplace had been subjected to bullying within the previous twelve months.[6]

Japan – From April 2010 to March 2011, 246, 907 civil individual labour disputes were taken to court of which 39,405 cases related to bullying and harassment, according to the Ministry of Health, Labour, and Welfare.[7]

United Kingdom – The British Crime Survey (BCS) gathers comprehensive data about workplace violence. The BCS estimated that 431,000 incidents of physical assaults and 418,000 incidents of threats occurred from 2002-2003 in England and Wales.[8] In 2011 a survey conducted by the UK's trade union UNISON, which represents the public service, found that six in ten workers in the UK had been bullied or had witnessed bullying in the past six months.[9] In the 2011 survey, more than half of the staff said that they were too scared to raise concerns and would stay in their job and suffer in silence, compared with only a quarter of staff who said they would stay when they were surveyed in 2009.

United States of America – The National Crime Victimisation Survey (NCVS) conducts an annual nationwide household survey of more than 100,000 individuals, who were at work or on duty. According to the NCVS, an average of 1.7 million violent victimisation workplace assaults took place during the period 1993 to 1999.[10]

In 2004, the U.S. National Institute for Occupational Safety and Health (NIOSH) completed a comprehensive survey on the prevalence of workplace bullying. The survey, which collected data from respondents in private and public organisations, found that 24.5 percent reported some degree of bullying in the preceding twelve months.[11] A survey conducted in 2010 by the Workplace Bullying Institute (WBI) found that 35 percent of the U.S. workforce, or an estimated fifty-three million Americans reported being bullied currently or at some time during their working life.[12]

Occupational Group Surveys
No country, sector, or occupational group can realistically claim to be free of workplace aggression and violence. However, surveys suggest that although the impact of workplace bullying is felt by countless millions around the globe, some occupations are more vulnerable and at higher risk than others.

The Health Sector
A study of the health sector, which was conducted by the World Health Organisation, the International Labour Organisation, the International Council of Nurses, and Public Services International, reported its findings in 2002. The survey was conducted across seven countries, including Australia, Brazil, Bulgaria, Lebanon, Portugal, South Africa, and Thailand.[13] The survey reported that psychological and physical violence was experienced in large numbers by employees in the health sector. In Bulgaria, the survey found that 7.5 percent of respondents reported being physically assaulted in the previous twelve months. In Brazil and the Lebanon, approximately 6 percent reported being physically assaulted; 10.5 percent reported being assaulted in Thailand and 17 percent in South Africa. When interviewed about psychological violence, 39.5 percent of respondents in Brazil said they experienced verbal abuse in the previous twelve months; in Bulgaria, the figure was 32.2 percent. The figure was 52 percent in South Africa, and 47.7 percent of respondents reported verbal abuse in Thailand. In the Lebanon, the figure was 40.9 percent, and up to 67 percent had reported verbal abuse in

Australia. In Britain, a report from the BCS in 2002–2003 also found that occupations with the highest risk of assault were police officers at 12.6 percent followed by health and social welfare professionals with a 3.3 percent risk factor.[14]

Right across the globe, health professions were found to have particularly high rates of bullying, not least because of the unique characteristics associated with this sector. Contributory factors included the crossover of the external environment into the workplace, which brought a wide variation of unpredictable emotions. These emotions gave the appearance of legitimate reasons for penetrating workplace boundaries, and staff became at a higher-than-average risk of inappropriate and violent conduct. In Scotland, the 2005 Emergency Workers Scotland Act provides protection to emergency hospital staff when they are on duty. Section 5 of the act states: It is an offence to assault or impede registered medical practitioners, registered nurses, or midwives acting for the Scottish Ambulance Service, within the hospital premises.[15]

The Teaching Sector

According to Verdugo and Vere, teachers in the United States were victims of some 1,708,000 nonfatal crimes at school during the 1995–1999 academic years. These included 1,073,000 thefts and 635,000 violent crimes (rape or sexual assault, robbery, and aggravated or simple assault). On average, these figures translated to about seventy-nine crimes per one thousand teachers per year.[16]

The Self-Employed

Interactive communications and the development of technology have improved direct advertising and sales, which has led to an increase in outsourcing and subcontracting work. This has led to an increase in the number of people who now work alone, and an increase in the number of people who are self-employed. Clients and customers can perceive operators working alone as an easy target for directing unwanted conduct and physical threats of violence. When this is combined with cash payments, motivated offenders have started to direct increased levels of violent aggression at operators, such as taxi drivers, petrol pump attendants, beauty therapists, doctors, dentists, and bus drivers.

Conclusions

These surveys indicate national representative estimates of bullying behaviour in the workplace, which showed considerable variations between countries, and even more striking variations between occupational groups. Caveats are issued against making any cross-sectional comparisons between countries or between occupations, as huge variations in methodologies for reporting and collecting data have made comparisons in the majority of cases totally incompatible.

Surveys help to increase an awareness of bullying behaviour and draw attention to the extent of the problem but do not provide an accurate substitute for accounts that are statistically recorded. When first conducted, they signalled a starting point for discussions between unions, employer groups, and government representatives. They formed the basis for anti-bullying guidelines and the introduction of legislation to deal with the problem. In most countries, however, no official systems have been introduced to gather information on a regular basis, and no definition has been agreed, that allows comparative findings to be made between countries or occupations.

Chapter 7 ∾

European Surveys
Monitoring the Workplace

In addition to national and occupational group surveys conducted in the workplace, the European Foundation provides information, advice, and expertise on living and working conditions on the basis of comparative information, research, and analysis conducted across the European Union member states. A priority of the European Foundation is promoting the improvement of living and working conditions. Since 1990, the European Foundation has audited working conditions within EU member states, through the European Working Conditions Surveys (EWCS). The surveys are conducted approximately every five years, and statistics are gathered, formulated, and analysed from a broad cross-section of EU workers. The results are published on a country-by-country basis with the average EU figures compared with previous years. The audit's main focus is detailing the number of incidents of violence that is experienced between individual workers. Information on organisational, systems, management, and legislation, which might influence the outcome of negative psychosocial behaviour between individuals, are not audited or recorded in the surveys.

In 2005, the fourth EWCS survey conducted an analysis of the EU25 countries. The survey reported 5 percent or one in twenty workers in the EU being personally subjected to violence either from fellow workers or others. Under the category of "Bullying and Harassment" in the same EWCS survey, the average EU figure was also found to be 5 percent of the workforce or one in twenty workers, with an overall 17 percent average variation between countries.[1]

Fieldwork for the fifth EWCS survey took place in 2010 covering thirty-four countries.[2] The countries included the EU twenty-seven member states and Norway, together with EU non-member countries from the candidate countries: Croatia, the Former Yugoslav Republic of Macedonia, Montenegro, and Turkey, abbreviated as follows:

AT	Austria	FI	Finland	PL	Netherlands
AL	Albania	HR	Croatia	Pl	Poland
BE	Belgium	HU	Hungary	PT	Portugal
BG	Bulgaria	IR	Ireland	RO	Romania
CZ	Czech Republic	IT	Italy	SE	Sweden
CY	Cyprus	LV	Latvia	SL	Slovenia
DK	Denmark	LT	Lithuania	SK	Slovakia
DE	Germany	LU	Luxembourg	TR	Turkey
EE	Estonia	MK	Macedonia	UK	Britain
ES	Spain	MO	Montenegro	XK	Kosovo
EL	Greece	MT	Malta		
FR	France	NO	Norway		

The survey also included potential candidate countries Albania and Kosovo. Over forty-four thousand workers were interviewed, and findings were presented from individual EU member states and the remaining seven countries. The EU27 average figure was detailed and compared with the previous EU15 and EU12 average figures. Under the heading "Violence in the Workplace," significant questions were asked, that related to how employees were being treated.

Question on Physical Violence: Have you been subjected to physical violence at work in the past year?

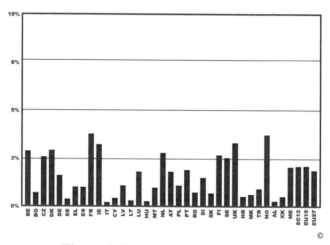

Figure 2. Physical Violence [3]
(Used with permission from the European Working Foundation)

The results of the surveys showed the levels of physical violence experienced by the working population ranged from 0.2 to 3.8 percent, giving a total variation between twenty-seven member states of 3.6 percent. The total EU27 average figure across the twenty-seven member states was 1.9 percent of the workforce. Comparing the EU27 average figure for physical violence in 2010 with the EU12 figure in 1991, the bar chart in figure 2 shows a percentage drop of 0.2 percent from 1991 to 2010. During this period, however, new member states joined the European Union, increasing the total workforce substantially with a corresponding increase in the number of workers exposed to physical violence.

Bullying and Harassment
The definition of bullying and harassment used in the EWCS surveys may indicate a difficulty when translations are used for pre-coded questions. The definition of bullying and harassment

that was used in the 2010 EWCS Survey was: "Bullying or harassment means harassing, offending, socially excluding someone or negatively affecting someone's work tasks. This could take form in the isolation of the person in the workplace, by voiding/nullifying his or her work, using threatening behaviour, telling stories behind his/her back, exerting on him/her some other form of mental pressure. This should occur repeatedly and regularly (e.g. weekly) and over a period of time (e.g., during about six months). These negative actions can be done by one or by more persons and usually the target of the bullying finds it difficult to defend his or herself against these actions."[4] Using the pre-coded definition above, the following question was asked.

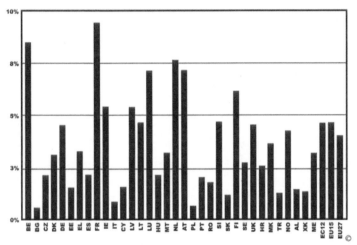

Figure 3. Bullying and Harassment [5]
(Used with permission from the European Working Foundation)

Question on Bullying and Harassment: Have you been subjected to bullying or harassment at work in the past year?

The survey found that the levels of bullying and harassment ranged from 0.6 percent to 9.5 percent of the workforce. This finding gave a total variation of 8.9 percent between the twenty-seven EU member states. The total average figure for the twenty-seven member states was 4.1 percent of the EU workforce who were subjected to being bullied or harassed. Comparing the EU27 average figure for bullying and harassment in 2010 with the EU12 figure in 1991, the bar chart in figure 3 shows a percentage drop of 0.8 percent from 1991 to 2010. With several new countries joining the European Union in the interim period, this corresponded to an overall increase in the total number of workers who experienced bullying and harassment across the European Union.

Question on Threats and Humiliating Behaviour: Have you been subjected to threats and humiliating behaviour at work in the last month?

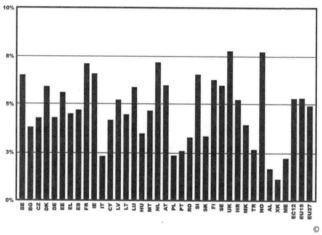

Figure 4. Threats and Humiliating Behaviour [6]
(Used with permission from the European Working Foundation)

The survey found the levels of threatening and humiliating behaviour in the previous month ranged from 1.2 to 7.8 percent, giving a total variation of 6.6 percent between the thirty-four countries. The total average EU27 figure for workers subjected to threatening and humiliating behaviour in the workplace across twenty-seven member states was found to be just under 5 percent. Comparing the EU27 average figure for threats and humiliating behaviour in 2010 with the EU12 figures for 1991, the bar chart in figure 4 shows a percentage drop of 0.4 percent from 1991 to 2010. As several new member states joined the European Union from 1991 and 2010, this figure reflects the addition of several million more EU workers who experienced threats and humiliating behaviour in the workplace.

Question on Verbal Abuse: Have you been subjected to verbal abuse at work in the last month?

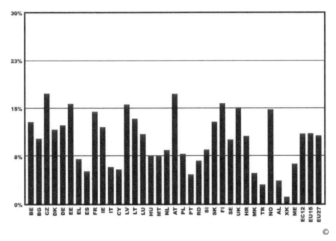

Figure 5. Verbal Abuse [7]
(Used with permission from the European Working Foundation)

The levels of verbal abuse ranged from 3.1 to 17.5 percent of the workforce, which gave a total variation between member states of 14.4 percent. The average EU figure across twenty-seven member states for verbal abuse in the month preceding the survey was 10.8 percent of the workforce. Comparing the EU27 average figure in 2010 with the EU12 average figures for 1991, the bar chart in figure 5 shows a percentage drop of 0.7 percent from 1991 to 2010. With a substantial increase in the EU workforce during the same period, this amounted to an increase in the number of employees who experiencing verbal abuse in the EU workplace.

Conclusion
The EWCS surveys conducted in 2010 highlighted some significant variations of 14.4 percent in the levels of psychosocial

behaviour recorded between member states. Strictly speaking, direct comparisons can only be made when all contributing factors are the same, which is not the case with EU member states. Striking variation exists because of differences in culture and disparity in perceptions of hostile and gendered violence. Legislation in place shows that behaviour condoned in one member state can be found to be completely unacceptable in another, and employees who are more aware of unacceptable behaviour can rate higher than those who tolerate abuses. The surveys conducted from 1991 to 2010 demonstrate that the average figures for physical violence, bullying and harassment, threats, humiliating behaviour, and verbal abuse have changed comparatively little (less than 1 percent) over two decades.

According to the 2007 annual report from the European Agency for Safety and Health, "significant changes taking place in the world of work may result in emerging psychosocial risks related to occupational safety and health." It reported these risks as being linked to the way work is designed, organized, and managed. The report outlined that increased levels of stress can lead to a serious deterioration of mental and physical health and that 22 percent of workers from twenty-seven member states believe that their health was at risk because of work-related stress.[8] The EWCS surveys, however, exclude all psychosocial risks that relate to how work is designed, organised, and managed. This focus effectively confines the EWSC surveys to a statistical measurement of the number of negative interactions experienced between workers on a one-on-one level. The surveys could be interpreted as meaning a lot of unavoidable conflict took place between staff, for no apparent reason. The surveys limit the scope of the findings, by excluding workplace practices and legislation, which often provides the only context in which prevention and intervention can be mitigated. A comprehensive audit of member states to include the legislation in place, the organisational stress factors, and the level of absenteeism that result from bullying behaviour could be used to direct policy makers to tackle changes at primary level, which the EU has separately acknowledged as framing how behaviour is influenced.

Primary intervention is the most effective and cost beneficial stage of intervention, involving the introduction of regulations and procedures to prevent and manage hazards and risks that relate to unwanted conduct in the workplace.

Sharing the Problems and Not the Profit

Countries that share a common currency, open trade agreements, and provide equal opportunities in education, health, and welfare systems become crucially concerned with having equal standards apply to all participating countries. In the absence of unilateral standards to regulate psychosocial risks in the workplace, extreme variations and imbalances emerge on the rights owed to workers. Employees working in countries with reduced working conditions and no social or medical support schemes unavoidably seek relief through free movement arrangements to member states who provide these services. Competing for economic markets with unequal financial burdens in the provision of benefits and conditions for workers, results in the creation of unfair competition. In a bid to win investment and trade contracts, a cost advantage is allowed to countries providing reduced standards to workers. Countries providing medical and social supports to employees from other countries, also incur additional financial penalties.

Chapter 8 ⌒⌣
Successful Career Psychopaths

Hervey Milton Cleckley MD, an American psychiatrist and pioneer in the field of psychopathy, first provided an influential clinical description of a psychopath in the twentieth century as "a person having a lack of remorse and shame, who uses charm, manipulation, and intimidation mixed with mild to severe violence to satisfy their needs."[1]

Being bullied is an emotionally draining and psychologically damaging experience that is now established as creating an impact equally as traumatic as a physical assault.[2] Trapped in such a relationship, there is always the lingering hope that an appeal can be made on some level to the better nature and compassion of the bully. However, the experience of being bullied by someone who lacks the capacity to feel shame, remorse, or guilt must be a terrifying and chilling ordeal. Shame and guilt are conceptualised as an individual's social thermostat, which mediates the state of social relationships. When inappropriate behaviour takes place, shame and guilt pop up like red flags that scream stop. However, when the emotions of guilt and shame are not discharged, no alert signals are sent to indicate a need to stop. The individual's conscience does not function effectively, and no mechanism is in place to determine when unacceptable behaviour is pushed beyond acceptable levels.

Psychopaths live in all cultures. The relatively isolated Inuit of the Arctic viewed them as irredeemable and, in the past, dealt with them by shoving them off the ice floes. Typically, where inferior social structures and poor working conditions exist, the innate tendencies of psychopaths become more easily expressed. When respect and human rights are central to the functioning of operations, psychopathic traits are inclined to be less prevalent. Similarly, in workplaces where self-promoting, individualistic accomplishments are encouraged, psychopathic behaviour is more likely to thrive than in workplaces that favour respect, connectedness, and personal responsibility. Psychopaths, who are often seen as people who commit crimes and end up in prison, are becoming more likely to choose a career as the route to big pay-offs. Unlike regular criminals, who risk being put away for life in the pursuit of wealth and opportunity, career psychopaths follow the lucrative career route to set them up for life.

The word *psychopath* is derived from the Greek words *psych,* meaning soul or mind, and *pathos,* meaning suffering or disease. Hervey Milton Cleckley's book *Mask of Sanity* was published in 1941 and refers to the "mask" of normal functioning. This term was derived from Cleckley's observations and explanation of how people with major mental disorders, such as psychopaths, appear normal and even engaging while concealing a disorder. As far back as the 1940s, Cleckley proposed a checklist of sixteen distinguishable characteristics attributed to psychopaths.[3] These characteristics included superficial charm, an ability to manipulate, good intelligence, and an incapacity for love. This broadly translates into people with no conscience who are characterised by a total disregard for other people's rights. Psychopaths find it hard to display emotion and show little concern for the feelings of others.

Operating within institutional and corporate structures, psychopaths engage in sophisticated tactics to gain influence and demonstrate their power and control to manipulate others. When no obstacles to negative psychosocial behaviour are in place and little value is placed on how people are treated, the ruthless predatory behaviour of psychopaths can target and strike with deadly effects. Not suffering from the normal pangs of guilt and remorse, which might keep the average employee awake at night, psychopaths can lie pathologically to push a sale or clinch a deal. Cut-throat and competitive businesses turn a blind eye to this behaviour in favour of goals scored and deadlines achieved. As the number and intensity of battles for market share increases, companies churn out advertisements that list the characteristics of psychopaths as key requirements for fulfilling the entrance requirements for the job.

To deal with career psychopaths, employers have to know how to recognise them. However, no matter how good the screening process, psychopaths are designed to overcome most obstacles that present a threat to their success. It would be a mistake to think psychopaths can be spotted straight away. People are much more likely to be charmed and fooled by them. Psychopaths can operate undetected for years until they achieve some degree of power and control and then start to wield their will. Using friendships as contacts, humiliating people in public, and exploiting the good nature and weaknesses of others to their advantage, people eventually start to feel paranoid, trapped, and controlled. It's hard to beat them at their own game and when they achieve positions of power and dominance, they can strike terror into the very core of a person's perception of humanity. To make the situation worse, they are often highly respected and may only reveal their duplicity of character to a few unrelated people. They are "go-getters" who appear as natural leaders with drive and energy and usually have an impressive list of accomplishments and achievement. The paradox is that a person complaining about the behaviour of a psychopath might appear as an incompetent, jealous underachiever who cannot cope with the stress and demands of work. While milder forms of psychopathic behaviour might be useful if managed properly, moderate to severe psychopathic behaviour could drive a target out of their mind—or their job.

In 1980, a revised checklist of distinguishable psychopathic characteristics was produced by psychologist Robert D. Hare. The Psychopathy Checklist, Revised (PCL-R) is now a recognised standard used by experts in assessing psychopathy. Studies conducted by Robert D. Hare in the 1970s are considered classics in psychopathic research academia. One such study was conducted with a sample group who watched a timer countdown to zero.[4] A harmless but painful electric shock was administered when the timer reached zero, which the subjects were made aware of in advance. In anticipation of the shock, the sample group sweated as soon as the clock started. Psychopaths, however, did not perspire but appeared to tune out and be fearless. This response can translate into people who have no learned or preconceived fear and are able to block out any impending or immediate unpleasantness. The absence of these normal physiological responses to fear, which constrain the behaviour of most people, can facilitate psychopaths behaving outside the norm. Without the typical impairments to fear and stress, such as rapid heartbeat, sweating, dry mouth, and trembling that tend to inhibit the majority of people conducting risky or unpleasant conduct, psychopaths in stressful occupations can ironically appear to be brave—even courageous—in the face of adversity and unpleasantness. As studies increasingly report, work-related stress as being a major health and safety issue in the workplace.[5]

It would seem that by joining these isolated dots together, a diagnosis of psychopathy might fit well in competitions for stressful jobs, and meet the entrance requirements needed to cope with this new occupational workplace hazard.

In 2005, psychologists Belinda Board and Katarina Fritzon of Surrey University gave personality tests to senior business managers, chief executives, psychiatric patients, and hospitalised offenders. The sample groups were then compared for profile overlaps. In their article "Disordered Personalities at Work," featured in the Psychology, Crime and Law journal, the authors describe some successful business people as holding some of the same characteristics as psychopaths. Relative to the patient sample groups, *histrionic* personality traits were found to be significantly higher in the senior management group's score. Relative to the patient sample groups, *narcissistic* and *compulsive* personality traits were found to be statistically the same as the management group's score.[6] At a descriptive level, *histrionic* characteristics, which included manipulativeness, superficial charm, insincerity, and egocentricity, were more likely to be characteristic of the management group than the patient groups. Narcissistic behaviour, such as grandiosity, lack of empathy, exploitativeness, independence, and *compulsive* behaviour, such as perfectionism, excessive devotion to work, rigidity, stubbornness, and dictatorial tendencies, were found to be equally common to all the groups sampled. The senior managers group was found less likely to demonstrate physical aggression or any other personality disorder traits by comparison to the sample groups.

Psychopaths can be attracted to large organisations where a bigger pool of people can be drawn to weave their web. They work hard at appearing normal and, at face value, are patient, accommodating, and well-dressed. They come across as charming and friendly, often showing a great interest in getting to know people they just met. For the person lavished with attention and charm, this can lead to a false sense of flattery and comfort, resulting in secrets, fears, and worries being effortlessly disclosed with no knowledge that these are the commodities psychopaths deal in. These commodities can later be used by the psychopath to exploit, betray, and lie to yield the psychopath's desired results. The indifferent and risk-taking environments adopted by many organisations can satisfy the slippery psychopaths' ability to be master manipulators of situations and the weak minded. They can live off the labours of others, playing cruel games to satisfy a variety of desires through power and control. If a threat or barrier is placed in the way of a psychopath, it is quite likely to end in a disastrous encounter. It could result in loss of promotion, career, friendships, marriage, and even custody battles. Low self-esteem is not a character flaw they possess and they usually have a grandiose and quite convincingly inflated sense of self-worth. Robert D. Hare remarked that "there are more narcissists in the business world than in the criminal population."[7] They may be somewhat crazy, but not stupid and are more likely to get promoted than caught.

While the key behavioural features of psychopaths have been defined to a great extent, physical characteristics associated with the behaviour are still being explored. In conjunction with neuroscience, magnetic resonance imaging (MRI), and psychological assessments studies, there is a suggestion that there is a neuro-developmental basis for psychopathic disorders. Research by clinical neuroscientists have found physical abnormalities in brain structures, such as the corpus callosum,[8] which may suggest that brain structures implicate abnormalities in the etiology of psychopathic and anti-social behaviour.

Other studies using MRI techniques compared sixteen unsuccessful psychopaths (caught offenders) with twelve successful psychopaths (uncaught) and twenty-three control subjects. Unsuccessful psychopaths showed exaggerated structural hippocampal symmetry (right greater than left) relative to the successful psychopaths group and the control subjects. This study was the first brain imaging analysis of successful and unsuccessful psychopaths. The studies concluded that structural hippocampal abnormalities in unsuccessful psychopaths may reflect an underlying neuro-developmental abnormality, resulting in poor contextual fear conditioning and insensitivity to clues predicting capture.[9] These studies suggest that transmission rates and faulty wiring, together with physical and asymmetrical differences, may form a basis for psychopathic and anti-social behaviour.

When Different Psychological Profiles Meet

A large combination of psychological profiles can give rise to a wide range of interactions that can lead to dysfunctional behaviour. In most communities, power differentials are authorised through legitimate control that allows some people formal charge over others. This can develop into the hierarchical bullying, of subordinates by people who are in positions of power. Personal, psychological, financial, and social strengths can also give rise to informal power differentials, which can result in lateral or horizontal bullying between peers, pupils, neighbours or friends. Strong capable individuals, often more competent, better paid, and more qualified, can also be bullied by people in less powerful formal positions, which gives rise to subordinates who bully bosses, pupils who bully teachers and children who bully parents, which is referred to as vertical bullying.

In addition to formal and informal power differentials, subclinical psychopaths, narcissists, sociopaths, and many other undiagnosed psychological conditions populate communal environments. These differences in psychological profiles can all lead to a patchwork of different interactive patterns of behaviour, some of which are compatible, while others can be potentially dangerous and distracting. Nevertheless, they all emphasise the need for educational and training awareness on what is acceptable and unacceptable behaviour in communal areas. These potential ticking time bombs support the introduction of regulations into communal areas to discourage injurious, careless, risky, and cruel behaviour. It supports a growing need to introduce anti-bullying legislation to protect individuals from potential dangers that can lurk in communal environments where mixed psychological profiles meet.

Chapter 9 ∽
Global Legislation on Bullying

Martin Luther King Jr. once said, "It may be true that the law cannot make a man love me, but it can keep him from lynching me, and I think that's pretty important."[1]

Explicit forms of aggression, such as physical assaults are regulated under the criminal justice system, providing legal protection and penalties to dissuade perpetrators from such behaviour. These sanctions, however, rarely apply to perpetrators of more covert forms of aggression, such as bullying. In most communities, sanctions are generally called up under the general "duty of care," where taking appropriate measures to protect against unwanted conduct is often implied rather than defined. Legislative measures to deal with covert forms of aggressive conduct are generally confined to the workplace, which are dealt with in this chapter.

Traditionally, protection in the workplace referred to protection from physical or chemical hazards, which presented an eminent or potential risk to the health and safety of employees.

Occupational health and safety legislation emerged to regulate and reduce these risks, and occupational health and safety authorities were set up to monitor and inspect workplaces to ensure these standards were met. As the interconnectedness between the more covert forms of violence were increasingly shown to result in trauma, which was equal and in some cases more extensive than physical acts of aggression,[2] some countries responded by dealing with psychosocial risks under existing health and safety legislation. In other countries specific legislation was introduced to deal with specific groups of employees, and specific situations where unwanted conducted took place. Specialised legislation to deal exclusively with the problem of negative psychosocial behaviour was introduced by countries, such as Belgium, Sweden, and Norway. In other countries, there is a complete absence of legislation with only assistance and support drawn from a range of voluntary charities and help lines.

Serious abuses of workers, such as sexual assaults and admissions to hospitals after employees jumped from upper story buildings to escape their place of employment, has led to intervention under human rights violations. At the Eighteenth World Congress on Safety and Health at Work in Seoul, Korea, in 2008, participants signed the Seoul Declaration on Safety and Health at Work, asserting that entitlement to a safe and healthy work environment was a fundamental human right.

Health and Safety Acts

When psychosocial risks are dealt with under health and safety legislation, the duty of the employer to protect employees against unwanted conduct can be outlined in general terms or can be specifically defined. Health and safety legislation, such as having "to ensure so far as is reasonably practicable, the health, safety and welfare at work of all employees,"[3] provides a very broad outline of the duty of the employer. When called upon to protect against unwanted conduct, such legislation can prove to be a very weak shield. In practice, negative psychosocial behaviour dealt with under health and safety legislation can prove of little value, if illnesses that result from bullying behaviour, such as stress are not included on the national official occupational health and safety list of illnesses or diseases. Not being "officially listed" excludes stress-related-illnesses being subject to the statutory requirements of being notified to the Occupational Health and Safety authorities (OHS). This exclusion results in illnesses arising from bullying behaviour not being subject to risk assessments or audit controls, in the same way as "officially listed" illnesses arising from physical or chemical hazards.

Cumulatively, this legislation results in the inclusion of unwanted conduct as a health and safety problem but excludes the behaviour from audits and controls under ancillary health and safety regulations that would facilitate the behaviour being reduced or eliminated. Regulating psychosocial behaviour under this legislation effectively depends on the strength of the legislation to specifically define psychosocial behaviour and its capacity to deal inclusively with the behaviour as a health and safety risk hazard.

Criminal Law

Bullying behaviour is not illegal and is not in itself a crime. If the behaviour results in the person becoming repeatedly pestered, experiencing menace, or being stalked, the behaviour can escalate into an offence under criminal acts against stalking and pestering, and a statement can be made to the police to seek to have the perpetrator cautioned. If criminal charges follow, the behaviour must be of a significant degree to fall within the scope of the criminal act, and victims must be in fear for their safety. Criminal legislation usually extends to behaviour that occurs in most locations, including the workplace. Individuals convicted of an offence under these laws are subject to the criminal justice system and can be charged with an offence and serve a prison term or fine.

Specific Legislation

Legislation that applies to specific groups of people or specific circumstances, is usually dealt with by specialised institutions and staff, who provide supportive avenues outside the main legislative process to deal with these disputes. In Europe in particular, there is a continuing trend towards the enactment of specific legislation to provide solutions. Examples of specific legislation include disability, sexual harassment, non-discrimination, equality, and unfair dismissal legislation.

Law against Discrimination/Equality Acts: This legislation is targeted toward providing protection against behaviour conducted on specific status-based grounds. National legislation applying the principals of equality and non-discrimination are generally adopted from the International Convention 111,[4] which was introduced by the International Labour Organisation (ILO) to address discrimination on certain protected grounds. These grounds include discrimination against specific groups of people because of their unique status, such as race, colour, sex, religion, political opinion, national extraction, or social origin.

Harassment: The word harassment is often interchanged with the word bullying, but in some countries harassment is specifically defined in legislation. Under the national domestic laws of some countries and under European Union Directives, specific provision is made against unwanted conduct that is specifically referred to as harassment and defined on certain grounds. In article 2 (3) of the Directive 2000/78/EC, the principles of equal treatment practices are implemented, which outlaws harassment on the grounds of religion or belief, disability, age, or sexual orientation. Article 2 (3) of the EU Directive 2000/43/EC outlaws harassment on the basis of racial or ethnic origin, and article 2 (1) (c) of the Directive 2006/54/EC refers to harassment on the grounds of unwanted conduct directed at the sex of a person. Under this specific legislation harassment is defined as unwanted conduct under the defined grounds listed above, which takes place with "the purpose or effect of violating the dignity of a person, and of creating an intimidating, hostile, degrading, humiliating or offensive environment."[5]

Sexual Harassment: Sexual harassment includes legislation specifically related to unwanted conduct that is directed at people because of their sex. The EU Directive 2002/73/EC enacted in September 2002 implements the principles of equal treatment for men and women relating to access to employment, vocational training, promotion, and working conditions. The directive introduced the concept of harassment related to sex, stating that it is a form of discrimination and a violation of the equal treatment principles.[6] The Directive 2002/73/EC replaced Directive 76/207/EEC and amended the definition of sexual harassment in article 2.(2) to include "where any form of unwanted verbal, non-verbal or physical conduct of a sexual nature occurs, with the purpose or effect of violating the dignity of a person, in particular when creating an intimidating, hostile, degrading, humiliating or offensive environment."[7] Across the globe, sexual harassment legislation has been introduced by most countries under equality or sexual harassments acts.

Unfair Dismissals: Employees who are bullied repeatedly in the workplace and fail to resolve these incidents may be forced to leave their employment and take a constructive or wrongful dismissals claim under unfair dismissals legislation. This legislation protects employees against being dismissed through wrongful or constructive means. Of particular relevance to bullying is the concept of constructive dismissal. Employees are constructively dismissed when they voluntarily leave their employment because the employer breached an express or implied term of the employment contract. In the United States, the doctrine in law is different and starts from the presumption that workers not expressly hired by a collective bargaining agreement or an individual employment contract are presumed to be "at will." That is, the employer is free to discharge individuals "for good cause, or bad cause, or no cause at all." In this employment relationship, the employee is equally free to quit, strike, or otherwise cease work.[8]

Specialised Legislation
Legal remedies that specifically deal with bullying behaviour may be sought under legislation, which can include equality, common, human rights, environmental, criminal, civil, anti-discrimination,

and constitutional law. The nature of the dispute will determine whether these remedies can be applied separately or if a combination of remedies is appropriate.

Australia – Australia operates a federal system of government with legislative variations between its six states. Two acts, namely the Occupational Health and Safety Act 1991 and the Safety, Rehabilitation, and Compensation Act 1988, originally administered health and safety issues. In January 2012, the Work Health and Safety Act 2011[9] came into affect replacing the 1991 Occupational Health and Safety Act. The act harmonised health and safety laws across Australian states and sets out to ensure a Person Conducting a Business or Undertaking (PCBU) has an obligation to provide safe and healthy workplaces against potential risks to the health and safety of employees. The act was accompanied by new codes of practice and health and safety regulations. Comcare was set up in 2011 to jointly partner workers, employers, and unions and to keep official records of incidents of bullying in the workplace.

Belgium – The Act of 4 August 1996 defines the requirements of employers to take the necessary measures to promote the well-being of workers in the performance of their work and lists the general obligations of workers.[10] The act of 1966 was modified on June 11, 2002, through amendments relating to protection from violence, including physical violence, verbal aggression, bullying, mobbing, and sexual harassment. On May 17, 2007, the Royal Decree addressed the psychosocial load caused by work, including violence, moral harassment (bullying), and sexual harassment.[11] The psychosocial load caused by work is defined as: any load of a psychosocial nature, which is caused by the execution of the work or arising as a result of the execution of the work, which has a detrimental effect upon the physical or mental health of the person. The general principles to determine and evaluate the risks by the employer are outlined in the decree.

Canada – A federal system of government operates in Canada with each of the ten provinces having responsibility for the regulation of occupational health and safety. The Canadian Labour Code also consolidated and addressed particular risk factors affecting health and safety at work.[12]

Individual provinces, which include Saskatchewan, Quebec, Manitoba, and Ontario, have their own anti-bullying laws. Quebec introduced the Workplace Psychological Prevention Harassment Act.[13] In section 2(a) psychological harassment is defined as "any vexatious behaviour in the form of hostile, inappropriate and unwanted conduct, verbal comments, actions or gestures that affects an employee's dignity or psychological or physical integrity." It states that every employee has a right to a work environment free from psychological harassment. The Ontario Bill 168 made amendments to the Occupational Health and Safety Act prohibiting vexatious comments and conduct against a worker known to be unwelcome.[14]

Denmark – In Denmark, the Consolidated Danish Working Environment Act 2005 requires employers to provide a safe and healthy working environment that at any time should be in accordance with the technical and social development of society.[15] The act requires employers to execute workloads in a way that does not affect the psychological health of the workforce.

Finland – The educational and industrial strategy in Finland is based on building an "information society." The Occupational Safety and Health Act 2002 outlines the appropriate safety arrangements and equipment needed to prevent or restrict violence.[16] The act deals with changes in working life and directs employees towards staying longer in work, where retirement is currently just under the age of sixty. Threatening situations are dealt with under section 27 of the act stating that threats must be considered in advance and the employer must draw up procedural instructions for controlling these situations. Practices in place for controlling or restricting the effects of violent incidents must be available and presented.

France – In response to the increasing gravity and extent of violence in the workplace, new provisions were introduced under the French Social Modernisation Law 2002, which specifically defines sexual and moral harassment.[17] Moral harassment states that no employee should be a victim of any repeated act of harassment on behalf of the employer or its representatives. The act states that no employee should suffer from any person who abuses the authority attributed by that individual's functions, which may be harmful to the employee's basic dignity or make working conditions humiliating or degrading or affect an employee's health or career. The Labour Code defines the duties and obligations of employers to introduce all measures necessary to prevent moral harassment. Criminal sanctions under the labour and penal code can be imposed with an imprisonment term of up to one year and a fine of up to €15,000, if a breach of the act occurs.

Ireland – The Safety Health and Welfare at Work Act 2005 regulates health and safety in the workplace.[18] Section 8. 2.(b) of the act outlines the employers obligation: as managing and conducting work activities in such a way as to prevent, so far as is reasonably practicable, any improper conduct or behaviour likely to put the safety, health, or welfare at work of his or her employees at risk. The act is accompanied by guidelines that do not form part of the subsidiary regulations. The guidelines are not legally enforceable, and failure to implement them is not a breach of the Safety Health and Welfare at Work Act. The authority responsible for issuing the guidelines is the Health and Safety Authority, who are entrusted to monitor whether employers are implementing satisfactory policies in line with these guidelines. The authority monitors the practices of employers through inspections and is dependent on how well the authority is financially resourced.

Netherlands – The Working Conditions Act 1999 defines employment related psychosocial pressure in section 3(e) as: sexual intimidation, aggression and violence, aggravation, and pressure of work in the employment situation that causes stress.[19]

New Zealand – Under the Health and Safety in Employment Act 1992,[20] employers have a legal duty to take all practical steps to ensure the safety of employees while in the workplace. This act includes protection from physical or mental harm caused by work-related stress. Protection is also provided under the Harassment Act 1997.[21] This legislation provides protection against the civil and criminal actions of stalking and harassment, for conduct that occurs on at least two occasions and covers harassment in the workplace and other locations.

Norway – The Working Environment Act 2009 outlines in section 1–1(a) the commitment of the Norwegian government to affording full safety from harmful physical and mental influences and operating a standard of welfare at all times consistent with the level of technological and social development in society. Section 4–2.2 outlines that working conditions must be arranged to allow workers reasonable opportunities for professional and personal development through their work. Work must be organised to provide varied content and contact with other people. In planning work schedules, section 4–2.2 (c) outlines how workers must be given an opportunity for professional responsibility and self-determination. Employees have the right not to be subject to harassment or improper conduct in the workplace.[22]

Sweden – The National Board of Occupational Safety and Health issued two ordinances in 1993 on workplace violence under the Work Environment Act.[23] The ordinances deal with violence and menaces (AFS 1993:2) and victimisation in the workplace (AFS 1993:17). They include a combination of preventative strategies at organisational and environmental levels. The act requires employers to plan and organise work in ways that remove hazards as far as possible and ensures that violence of any form is not tolerated, whether as a risk or a threat. The ordinances highlight the importance of the work environment and outline the key role of work organisation to provide employees with comradeship, social support, work, and the opportunity for personal and social contact.

United Kingdom – The UK Health and Safety at Work Act 1974 provides a legal duty on employers to ensure the health, safety, and welfare of employees.[24] Additional protection against unwanted conduct is provided under the Protection from Harassment Act 1997.[25] This legislation was introduced largely in response to stalking offences but was later used as grounds for relief in bullying cases. The act carries both civil and criminal liabilities against perpetrators who engage in conduct on at least two occasions that amounts to harassment of another person whom the perpetrator knows or ought to know amounts to harassment. The court has the power to grant a restraining order after a person is convicted. Section 5 of the act outlines offences and punishments that can carry up to five years in prison, a fine, or both. While the legislation is not directed specifically to violence at work or school, it is of sufficient breadth to apply to harassment in most locations.

The United States – A federal system of government operates in the United States with each state introducing its own additional or individual legislation. Nationally, the Occupational Safety and Health Act 1970 [26] legislates for occupational safety and health in the workplace. The legislation is accompanied by guidelines, which do not form part of subsidiary regulations. The guidelines are not legally enforceable, and failure to implement the guidelines is not a breach of the Occupational Safety and Health legislation. The authority responsible for issuing guidelines is the Occupational Safety and Health Administration. The authority is entrusted with monitoring employers to ensure that they implement satisfactory policies in line with these guidelines. Monitoring employers is dependent on how well the authority is financially resourced. Under state law, the Healthy Workplace Bill is being introduced as a model to regulate health and safety in the workplace and is currently in the process of being adopted by approximately twenty-one states.[27]

European Law – In the European Union, issues about health and safety have been on the agenda since the Treaty of Rome in 1957. In 1989 the Framework Directive 89 / 391 / EEC was introduced to provide an enabling framework for member states to provide more detailed decrees of safety. Article 1.1 of the directive gave a broad commitment "to introduce measures to encourage improvements in the safety and health of workers at work." Article 5 of the directive imposes a general provision on employers to "ensure the safety and health of workers in every aspect related to the work."[28] The directive gave a commitment to "developing a coherent overall prevention policy, which covers technology, organisation of work, working conditions, social relationships, and the influence of factors related to the working environment."[29] The response by member states for transposing the EU directive into national domestic law was fragmented with striking legislative variation being adopted within member states. Almost ten years after the framework directive was issued, it came in for criticism within the European Union itself. In 1997, the European Commission issued findings in a publication entitled *Guidance on the Prevention of Violence at Work*. The publication included a review of the existing EU literature, guidelines, and draft guidance plans pertaining to violence at work and a survey on the prevalence of violence. The findings stated "the existence of guidelines to deal with violence was not uniform across the EU."[30] It stated that "in the absence of guidelines, it was unlikely that consistent and comprehensive management of the issue actually takes place."[31] It reported "the implementation of legislation must be questioned."[32] It concluded that, it is likely the "operation of legislation in the area is somewhat less than optimal,"[33] and that there was "considerable room for improvement in the management of this issue at all levels."[34]

In 2001, the European Commission's Advisory Committee on Safety, Hygiene, and Health Protection at Work pursuant to Article 6 of the framework directive 89/391/EEC) stated:

—The committee urges the Commission to draft guidelines based on an essentially preventive approach, starting from a definition of the phenomenon in all its various forms and determination of the risk factors that employers are obliged to assess under the terms of the Framework Directive.

This initiative should also be accompanied by an awareness raising campaign to draw more attention to the problem and to the need to head off violence at work.[35]

Following these suggestions, the European Union issued a communication in 2001, entitled *Adapting to Change in Work and Society: A New Community Strategy on Health and Safety 2002–2006.*[36] The strategy called for adapting the legal framework to cover the emerging psychosocial risks. It stated in paragraph 3.3.2:

—The "increase in psychosocial problems and illnesses are posing a new challenge to health and safety at work and are compromising moves to improve well-being at work. The various forms of psychological harassment and violence at work likewise pose a special problem nowadays, requiring legislative action. Any such action will be able to build on the acquis of recently adopted directives rooted in Article 13 of the EC Treaty, which define what is meant by harassment, and makes provision for redress."[37]

  —In their 2007 annual report, the European Agency for Safety and Health, reported on the annual economic cost of work-related stress in the EU15, which was estimated to be €20,000 million.[38]

  —The 1989 EU Directive 89/391/EEC is currently in place to regulate health and safety issues in the EU workplace and the findings remain relevant.

The United Nations
The Universal Declaration of Human Rights proclaimed by the General Assembly on December 10, 1948, asserts in Article 1 that "all human beings are born free and equal in dignity and rights."[39] This article has always been recognised as articulating a common definition of human value that is sacred. From 1949 until 1976, the Universal Declaration of Human Rights stood alone as an international standard of achievement for all people of all nations. Several decades later, many argue that a gap stands

between the guarantee of "dignity" in Article 1 and the delivery of "dignity" into the everyday lives of people.

The International Labour Organisation (ILO)

The ILO is the agency of the United Nations that deals with labour standards in the workplace. It is a tripartite agency bringing together representatives from government, employer, and employee groups. Their function is to jointly shape policies and programmes that promote decent work for all. A guiding principle of the ILO as outlined in the Declaration of Philadelphia is that labour is not a commodity.[40] To formulate its labour standards, the ILO draws up conventions. It also draws up a list of occupational diseases that reflect the latest developments in the identification and recognition of occupational diseases. According to the ILO protocol 155, an occupational disease covers "any disease contracted as a result of an exposure to risk factors arising from work activity."[41] To date stress has not been included on the ILO official list of occupational diseases. In March 2010 the ILO "revised list" of occupational diseases included post-traumatic stress disorder (PTSD) and "mental and behavioural disorders." This list was the first international acknowledgement of psychosocial illness's having any associated links with occupations and behaviour in the workplace. To date no ILO convention exists to make preventative measures a requirement for businesses or institutions as part of their duty of care or guardianship. No convention has been introduced to ensure against unwanted behaviour being included as an offence against *all* children and *all* adults to safeguard their health and well-being.

The World Health Organisation

The WHO was established in 1948 as an agency of the United Nations. It has responsibility for providing leadership on global health matters, shaping the health research agenda, setting norms and standards, and monitoring and assessing health trends. In 2002, the WHO launched the first World Report on Violence and Health. As a health issue affecting millions of workers, stress has not made it onto the official list of occupational illnesses, which is promoted by the WHO as adversely affecting health. The WHO has defined violence universally as being "the intentional use of physical force or power, threatened or actual, against oneself, another person, or against a group or community, which either results in or has a high likelihood of resulting in injury, death, psychological harm, maldevelopment or deprivation."[42]

Unilateral Solutions

To transcend the wide variation in standards that apply to psychosocial risk behaviour internationally, countries look beyond the limitations of national jurisdictions. Individual countries seek international agreement on a definition of bullying. Individual countries look for international regulations and solutions to outlaw unwanted conduct that applies unilaterally to all individuals, who now operate and work in what is a single global economic working environment.

Chapter 10 ﹏
Making a Civil Claim

Cases of bullying taken to court are usually charged with human and moral wrongdoing, which are often accompanied with financial and personal injustices. Unfortunately, taking a claim does not mean that justice will necessarily be served in court or that redress will be found within the legal system. A body of rights, obligations, and remedies are applied by courts in civil proceedings known as tort law, which provides relief for those who suffer harm from the wrongful acts of others as a result of *tortuous* conduct. The term tort comes from the Latin term torquere meaning "twisted or wrong," which allows an action to be brought by private citizens under civil proceedings. While one might be forgiven for believing that these laws would apply to the tortuous acts of bullying, the principles of negligence or intention, which are the standard redress in such cases, may not encompass bullying behaviour. In many cases of bullying, the attitude and excuse of aggressors is that their actions were not intended to be taken as offensive or hurtful. As bullying is not defined in statutes, individual cases of civil actions against perpetrators are difficult. Negligence on the part of the school, workplace, or cyber community may also prove difficult, if no defined duty of care exists, which specifies that intervention or preventative measures must be taken by the community to reduce or eliminate such actions. The essential element in any *tort* action is that the plaintiff must establish that the defendant was under a legal duty to act in a particular fashion and that the defendant breached this duty. An absence of any defined duty of care can often mean that only the most egregious actions causing the most catastrophic psychological damage result in even a threat of legal liability.

Those who suffer mental and physical health problems that follow from incidents of bullying will generally attribute these to their experience of being bullied. Increasingly, studies and research also confirm the interconnectedness between psychological violence and stress-related illnesses; however, this does not constitute unquestionable evidence in court. The plaintiff's must establish that they suffered an injury or loss as a direct result of certain actions. To pursue a valid claim, a substantial burden of proof will have to be presented to the court. The role of the court is to determine whether the defendant breached a legal obligation and to award financial remedies in accordance with any harm or loss suffered.

Taking a Civil Action
All legal claims are restricted by statutes of limitation, and cases must be taken within definite time frames. Claims should be submitted well before the expiry of these limitations and as soon as possible following the last incident of complaint. Court jurisdictions place a financial ceiling on the maximum amount of compensation that can be awarded. Depending on the financial claim being made, cases should be filed to the appropriate court. Constitutional actions must generally be brought before a higher court, regardless of the financial compensation being claimed, which will significantly increase legal costs.

A distinction is sometimes drawn between moral fault and legal fault. Persons who negligently or intentionally cause injury to others are often considered morally blameworthy for having failed to live up to an expected threshold of human conduct. On the other hand, legal fault is more of an artificial standard of conduct created by governments to protect society. The legal right to dignity, respect, and protection against unwanted conduct can be complex, generic, and diverse. In practice all cases of bullying vary considerably when all aspects are taken into account. A combination of actions may even be advisable. A personal injury claim, breach of employment contract, or a breach of constitutional law may need to be challenged. Criminal laws that legislate against pestering, stalking, and menace may be a solution, or offences under specific legislation, such as anti-discrimination may prove to be the most appropriate.

Cases of bullying may involve other complex questions touched on under health and safety practices, insurance, mental and physical health history, and relationship issues. In most cases, the victim must prove that the damages occurred and provide evidence to show that the damages resulted from the unwanted conduct of the defendant. If no definite legal duty exists on the part of the defendant, civil challenges are made lengthy, expensive, and profoundly difficult to establish. If the facts of the case go beyond the patchwork of legal remedies available, the case taken must be strained to accommodate the legal remedy in place. In these circumstances, interpreting negative psychosocial behaviour as a wilful or wanton intention to cause illness or injury to the victim is made difficult for both the victim and the courts.

Taking a claim can be emotionally difficult, especially if a plaintiff continues to suffer from the trauma of being bullied. Instead of receiving an apology or any acknowledgement, victims may get denials from the perpetrators with a strong defence that apportions blame on the victim. The defence may question the mental health of the victim, which may require proof to prove the contrary. Such a legal response may seem to lack any compassion, but this is a standard legal defence in court. Taking a civil case may often only serve to deepen the distress for victims compounding their hurt and pain in what might be a further personal assault. Previous precedents and awards made in case law within individual countries should serve to influence any decisions to take a legal action.

Claims are based on the evidence produced, and the burden of proof is determined on the balance of probabilities. Injuries sustained under psychological disorder claims generally show a second injury of a physical nature. These injuries can range from low-back pain, respiratory or digestive disorders, ulcers, heart problems, skin or speech conditions, hair loss, or other conditions brought on by stress. In support of a claim, a medical opinion is regarded by the court as a diagnosis of an illness. To establish a causal link between the health problems suffered and the negative behaviour experienced, a conclusive professional report in support of this causal link must be furnished to the courts by an occupational therapist, psychologist, or forensic psychiatrist.

The plaintiff needs to demonstrate with unequivocal evidence that their psychological well-being was damaged due to the actions and behaviour that they experienced. They need to show that they suffered a diagnosed condition of ill health to a degree that may need to qualify as a mental or behavioural disorder such as Post Traumatic Stress Disorder (PTSD). A counter and affirmative defence to any claim can be demonstrated by showing that all reasonable care was exercised to prevent the incident occurring. A counter defence is further supported by defendants by showing that any actionable behaviour was promptly corrected when the situation was brought to their attention.

Medical certificates giving generic reasons for absenteeism, such as stress, are not considered notification to the defendant that prompt corrective action must be taken. Medical certificates with a diagnosis of work or school-related-stress can be considered notification that requires attention and further action. Returning from an absence of work or school-related-illness, victims of bullying should include a letter of explanation, outlining the impact a particular situation had on their health, with a request for intervention to prevent any further reoccurrence.

To demonstrate that the psychological trauma suffered resulted from the experience of being bullied, victims may need to show that no contributory psychological factors existed in their lives at the time, which could have compounded or caused the trauma. The claimant may also need to show that no prior history of a psychological illness existed, which could have affected their condition. Evidence should be presented to the courts to show the defendant neglected to satisfy a request or statutory obligation to protect against unwanted conduct. Claimants must also show they made the defendant aware of the problem and gave the defendant every opportunity to remedy the situation, but singularly failed to do so. Claimants must show that they exercised the correct use of health and safety procedures to avoid any risk or threat to their own health. Calling on colleagues or peers as witnesses to support a claim can prove difficult, especially if witnesses remain in the same community as the bully. If no requirement exists to record incidents of bullying, it provides the defendants with control over their version of events after the fact. Peers and colleagues are unlikely to contradict the defendant's version and go to bat for the victim. In any event, contradictory evidence can amount to a she-says-he-says argument, which becomes a question of who is believed.

Cases are determined on the legal rights of the victim that were compromised. Financial compensation is awarded based on the culpability of the defendant, the severity of the injuries, and the loss and damages suffered. Each case is set down for hearing. Judgments are delivered, and financial compensation is awarded or denied. A decision on payment for legal costs is also given.

Personal Injury Claims

In cases of personal injury claims, the mental and physiological trauma suffered as a result of bullying behaviour is used as grounds for relief. The claimant is effectively trying to show that the ill health suffered from the impact of the negative psychological and emotional trauma was somewhat equivalent to the physical impact of an accident. A claim for compensation may be taken under employer or public liability insurance.

Employees seeking compensation are covered under public liability insurance. Other parties making a claim, such as students or clients are covered under public insurance liability, and notification of personal injury applications are returned to the policy holder and the insurance company. Settlement of claims can vary considerably, taking anything from a few months to several years. Early notification, served with medical reports, can result in insurance companies making early settlements to reduce legal court costs. In an effort to reduce the legal burden on both parties and provide the option of reaching an early settlement, some countries provide dedicated authorities that deal with personal injury claims. If no agreement is reached, the application can proceed through the courts. Social services or state-run occupational injury insurance schemes will sometimes provide financial relief, if the criteria for social insurance contributions are satisfied and the necessary medical certificates and reports are submitted.

The above explanations are general guidelines that provide a broad outline of a selected range of solutions. Before committing to any legal action, the case should be discussed with an informed and objective third-party. Information centres, trade unions, and anti-bullying centres provide advice and support. It is essential to consult a solicitor and preferably arrange a consultation with a junior or senior counsel who specialises in the area before deciding to proceed with a court challenge.

Chapter 11 ❧
Bullying of the Elderly

Bullying of the elderly is referred to under the generic name of *elder abuse*. The World Health Organisation defined elder abuse as "a single, or repeated act, or lack of appropriate action, occurring within any relationship where there is an expectation of trust which causes harm or distress to an older person."[1] This definition is broader than many others, having components that make it universally applicable to many communities, such as schools, workplaces, institutions, and social media sites. Distinguishing characteristics that separate it from other definitions include a lack of action through omission as being as damaging as abuse through commission. The definition also acknowledges that victims can become exposed to abuse within relationships where there is "an expectation of trust."

In cases of elder abuse, people in positions of trust would include spouses, partners, family members, friends, children, neighbours, and individuals attached to services, such as doctors, nursing home staff, and other caring professionals and service providers.

Until the 1970s, elder abuse had gone unrecognised, and many deaths attributed to natural, accidental, or undetermined causes have now been acknowledged by the World Health Organisation (WHO) as being a consequence of abusive or neglectful behaviour.[2] Up until 2002, five surveys conducted from the 1980s onwards were relied on to a great extent for insights, information, and statistics on elder abuse. The surveys, which were conducted in England, the United States, Canada, the Netherlands, and Finland found that between 4 to 6 percent of the elderly population reported being abused, when a range of abuses were considered.[3–7]

To highlight the prevalence of elder abuse, the United Nations designated June 15 as World Elder Abuse Awareness Day (WEAAD), which began in 2006. The day is increasingly marked by events held across the globe to raise awareness and provide safeguards against elder abuse. WEAAD calls on governments "to carry out more effective prevention strategies and stronger laws and policies to address all aspects of elder abuse." WEAAD also calls on governments "to optimize living conditions for older persons and enable them to make the greatest possible contribution to our world."[8] Ageing is not a disease and should not be seen as a problem but a natural part of the cycle of life. However, a considerable number of characteristics that define the natural cycle of ageing continue to be dealt with as though the ageing process unexpectedly took society by surprise. Many constraints that come with old age, such as reduced hearing, sight, mobility, isolation, and dependency on others have restricted many of the elderly population from extending their quality of life. Some countries responded by providing affordable services to adjust and remedy these natural physical restrictions that come with old age, while others have ignored the situation, and left it to the elderly population to find their own solutions.

Risk Factors of Elder Abuse
The typical risks associated with elderly abuse are many, and isolation is one of the most significant. Like many constraints that come with old age, the natural cycle of loss through deaths

and family members moving away can result in isolation. Community support networks have also weakened because of socioeconomic changes that further compound the possibility of isolation. Old age is not the problem, but being lonely as a result of isolation, can place elderly people into positions of vulnerability, if no substitute solutions are provided.

Negative perceptions created in society have to a large extent led to the stereotyping of elderly people. Stereotyping promotes elderly people as being incapable, dependant, and helpless. Symptoms associated with ageing, such as memory loss, impaired eyesight and reduced hearing are often exaggerated to illicit humour and poke fun, by portraying the elderly as doddery and confused old dears. These images, when exaggerated by TV programmes caricature elderly people as being weak, frail, and a nuisance. This caricaturing of the elderly is counterproductive and has often exposed elderly people to abuse by making them ready targets for discrimination, ageism, exploitation, and stigmatisation. It results in complaints made by elderly people being ignored, questions being fobbed off, and information being withheld. It creates a general consensus in society that allows a skewed version of reality to be presented to older people, rather than a factual account, as though their connection to reality expired or ran out. Stereotyping is often popularised and used to create deliberate confusion in the minds of elderly people. It can be used as a form of psychological abuse to make elderly people doubt their own memory and judgment. It can be a tactic relied on as an opportunity by motivated offenders to take financial advantage and trick elderly people into changing their wills or parting with money or valuables.

If there is no access to advocacy or third-party intervention, elderly people trying to seek help or stand up to this type of psychological abuse can feel compromised. They may find that they are up against a culture where they are considered an incapable species, with an accelerated incapacity to think clearly. Too easily, all attempts to explain the abuse is brushed off and dismissed, in the widely accepted belief that the elderly person is suffering from the cognitive impairments of old age. Services that can determine the quality of life of elderly people are often poor and inadequate and accompanied with lengthy form-filling procedures, which can add layer upon layer of stress to elderly people trying to access these services. The operation of inadequate services and the limitations of access often offer a much more accurate description of failures by policy makers, state institutions, and service providers to cater for the elderly rather than any incapacity on their part. Dates on birth certificates tell little about the capabilities, talents, or attitudes of the certified holders, and stumbling blocks to extending and improving the natural decline that old age brings are all too often inherent in the poor services provided.

Service providers in positions of trust can exploit the elderly by overcharging or providing less-than-optimal products or services. Such exploitation can include caregivers, home and general help, medical staff, and other professionals. An example of unscrupulous conduct can be seen with hearing aid providers who offer an essential aid to improving the quality of life for elderly people. Hearing devices imported for less than €100 can be sold to the elderly for €5,000 a pair. An EU 15927 standard applies to services offered by hearing aid professionals.[9] However, the standard has no legal status, and in many countries, hearing aid service providers remain unregulated.

Government grants for hearing aids amounting to millions are commonly provided for the elderly. Despite this financial outlay by the state, there is no watchdog agency exists to regulate the industry. The government grant is paid to the service provider after the device is fitted, and elderly clients are asked to pay any balance of monies owed up-front. A limited number of consultations follow to adjust the hearing requirements. If poor or inadequate services are given, no access is available to expertise other than the service provider. Left with no choice but to pursue a civil or consumer claim, the elderly person becomes anxious and frustrated with lengthy form-filling procedures, escalating costs and no operational hearing device. Unable to make progress, elderly people often give up and are left with a redundant government grant and a costly hearing device that does not enhance their hearing. The less-than-adequate service is precipitated due to a failure by governments to regulate the industry, which is then used by unscrupulous service providers to exploit the vulnerability of the elderly. The barriers created to making complaints against bad quality services perpetuate the exposure of the elderly to continued poor services. In the latter days of life, years filled with moments of work, respect, and love are easily forgotten in incidents such as this that wash away their expectation of respect.

As a social and political issue, national advocacy groups, unions, and legislation representing the rights of the elderly collectively demonstrate the presence or absence of concern at a national level. To date, most countries have not introduced legislation to specifically deal with the problem of elder abuse. Few protocols or safeguards exist within financial institutions to deal with or protect against financial abuses. Doctors and nurses, who are often best placed to witness cases of elder abuse, do not address the problem in their diagnoses as it is not included in their training. Protocols are not in place in hospitals or nursing homes to detect and deal with cases of suspected elder abuse as would apply to cases of child abuse. The lack of action and the absence of legislation to support and galvanise against these abuses, demonstrate a poor effort on the part of society to acknowledge the needs of this sector.

Some countries are much further advanced in providing a response to catering for old age and elder abuse than others. Some countries operate a fully integrated system of reporting elder abuse with dedicated public officials or an appointed Ombudsman who investigates all complaints and concerns that effect the elderly community. These services give a voice to the elderly population and help to highlight unacceptable behaviour by people in positions of trust as well as repeat offenders. National campaigns for creating awareness of elder abuse receive funding and expertise. Professional courses and qualifications covering ethical and legal issues associated with elder abuse are available for medical, social, and health-care practitioners, which enables professionals to conduct assessments, diagnosis and referrals for elder abuse.

Signs of Elder Abuse

- Complaining about certain people regularly, while praising others, especially new "best friends"
- Indications of being overly depressed and withdrawn, such as not getting dressed or performing basic tasks and never going out even when they can
- Inability to sleep or sleeping too much
- Appearing fearful of spending time away from their caregiver or family member, being afraid to make decisions or have discussions unless the caregiver or family member is present, being afraid to talk about a caregiver or family member
- Unpaid bills and no spending money, worried about money, bank statements not coming to the elder's home address, unusual activity in bank account statements, including withdrawals and the use of the ATM
- Seems to have too many accidents and falls
- Belongings or documents missing
- Suspicious signatures on checks or other documents

Physical Abuse

Typical physical abuse includes pushing or poking, restraining or confining an elderly person to a room or bed. Instances of physical abuse directed at elderly people where no precipitating resistance can be offered, describe abuse in terms that approach torment or cruelty.

Psychological or Emotional Abuse

Psychological and emotional abuse includes being persistently critical, shouting, swearing or humiliating a person; not facilitating friends, neighbours or relatives to visit; ridiculing their reduced capacity and dependency by constantly criticising and blaming them for the trouble they cause; and restricting their access to the full use of their home. Withholding information relating to social financial, and health matters is also emotionally abusive. Psychological and emotional abuse can also be nonverbal behaviour, such as silence, sulking, or shunning.

Financial Abuse or Exploitation

People over sixty years of age control a substantial percentage of the wealth in most countries, which when combined with a dependency or reduced capacity can make them attractive targets for motivated offenders. Fear and deception are often used by "trusted" relatives and friends to control finances. Coercion and manipulation can be used to secure inheritance, unauthorised use of a person's property, money, pension book, bank account, or other valuables. Elderly people can also become targets of a broad range of fraudulent scams attempted by calculating con artists and door-step criminals, who befriend, groom and try to extract lifesavings from the elderly. Unable to withstand the high pressure of promotion, canvassing, or claims that their homes are in the last stages of decrepitude, elderly people are often persuaded by their trusting nature, vulnerability, and isolation to make charges to credit cards or withdraw money for poor or unnecessary workmanship.

Abuse through Neglect

Neglecting to comfort or communicate with an elderly person or restricting essential medication or services are all forms of neglect that cause harm and distress. In the later stages of dependency, signs of neglect can be in the form of bedsores, open wounds, improper medical care, cuts, dehydration, malnutrition, over sedation, poor hygiene, weight loss, unwashed and uncombed hair, burns, and bowel impactions.

Rights Abuse

Rights abuses include manipulating or coercing elderly people into controlling their affairs on the basis of reduced capacity. A general absence of rights will arise as a result of poor legislation and an absence of advocacy and controls to deal with issues that affect the lives of the elderly. The presences of any of the above signs are not in themselves proof of bullying or abuse but should be a cause for concern and further enquiries.

Domestic Elder Abuse

Prior to 2002, surveys conducted on the elderly population were almost exclusively limited to the elderly population in domestic community settings. Elderly married males were found most likely to be abused by their spouses, adult children, and other relatives. This situation was also found to apply equally in the same proportion to elderly married women.[10] These findings were of benefit to understanding the problem of elder abuse but provided few strategies or protocols for intervention, as domestic elder abuse generally remains beyond the sphere of permitted outside influence.

Strained family relationships can often worsen over time as a result of stress and frustration caused by increased dependency. Family members who may have had a negative relationship with the elderly person may feel entitled to treat them badly. The relative or caregiver may have an accommodation or financial dependency on the care receiver, which becomes a source of conflict. Family members with financial problems or addictions, such as substance abuse, can direct abuse at the older person. Significant changes in technology have made managing finances more complicated for some elderly people who need to disclose financial details to others to assist them with transactions. When placed into positions of financial dependency, helpers, carer, or family members under financial stress may become motivated to seek financial benefit and opportunity.

Abuse in Nursing Homes

When the complications of old age increase, suitable arrangements for minding elderly parents and relatives can be limited. The provision of medical support systems and services that cater to minding elderly people in their own home and community may not be a viable option. In many cases people turn to the assisted-living arrangements of nursing homes as the only option available to continue the conscientious care families may no longer be able to provide. However, while many facilities provide this care, some do not. Documentaries investigating residential care facilities have highlighted one scandal after another, often culminating in nursing homes being forced to close. Media reports on elder abuse and incidents of neglect suggest that the policies in place fell well short of ensuring that basic guardianship standards were in place. The public watched on as no punishments or penalties followed from the criminal judicial system to prosecute the individuals running these homes, or those who conducted the abusive practices.

In the coming decades, a dramatic global increase in the older age segment of the population will be accompanied by an expected increase in nursing home residential care facilities. At the heart of this solution is the concern that nursing homes should be designed to go beyond bed, board, and nursing care and provide homes that are reflective of activities, therapies, social supports, and community interaction. Purpose-built homes springing up in the middle of nowhere charging $1,000 a week with little or no connection to the local community or much-needed facilities and social services have raised concerns. Nursing homes, which do not form part of the local community, have been referred to as the warehousing of the elderly. Many believe that, if nursing homes cannot be located within communities, an emphasis should be placed on elderly people being accommodated to remain in their own homes with assisted supports from their local community.

Despite the large number of elderly people now living in nursing homes, there is a lack of regulation and data on the level of care provided. Statistics are often absent, outdated, or scant with few national surveys commissioned on private or public nursing home care units. In a survey in the Unites States, 36 percent of nursing home staff reported witnessing at least one incident of physical abuse in the previous year. At least one incident of psychological abuse was observed by 81 percent of the sample surveyed in the preceding year, and 40 percent of nursing home staff admitted they had committed a psychological act of abuse against resident patients during the same period.[11] In the past, carers who were abusive to elderly people were dismissed as suffering from "caregivers stress." This excuse was held up as some type of legitimate explanation for the ongoing difficulties that caregivers had in coping with demanding elderly people. However, organisations that advocate the rights of the elderly suggest that these offenders have been wrongly conceptualised and should be characterised by the criminal intent they inflict on the elderly.

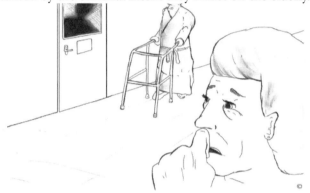

Abusive behaviour directed on a personal level toward residents in nursing homes can be accompanied by institutional abuses. Institutional abuses generally operate on the basis that the institutions seek to make larger financial profits by cutting back on the services they provide. Institutions maximising profits would typically pay low wages to staff, and operate a lower standard of care facilities. Financial cutbacks would also be reflected in under qualified staff, inadequate light or heating, a high staff turnover, and poor quality food. Other factors would include a lack of social interactive programs and social facilities. Vulnerable residents who can offer little resistance often become victims of both institutional and interpersonal abuse.

The provision of services in nursing homes generally includes the following:

- The rights of residents—access to information and consultation, encouragement to express views, consent to treatment and care, and the right to a written contract.

- Protection of residents—protection from bullying and all other abuse and safeguards around the handling of finances
- Health and social care needs—these include assessments of health, personal and social care needs, and contributions to care plans
- Quality of life—the exercise of choice, contact with visitors, and control over independence
- Staffing—this includes the qualifications and vetting of staff members and their supervision
- The Care Environment—this includes the physical environment and access to the outdoors, hygiene, and personal belongings
- Management and Governance—this includes policies on safety and well-being and a statement setting out the service provided by the care unit

Legislation

The Universal Declaration of Human Rights, which states that all human beings are born free and equal in dignity and rights,[12] does not change with age. The International Network for the Prevention of Elderly Abuse (INPEA) promotes the introduction of a UN convention to specifically define the rights of the elderly and emphasise their right not to be abused. The rights afforded to the elderly are based on the United Nations principles for older persons that were adopted by the UN General Assembly in December 1991. Under Resolution Number 46/91,[13] eighteen principals are listed. The heading of dignity listed under number seventeen, states that "older persons should be able to live in dignity and security and be free of exploitation and physical or mental abuse." This, resolution, however, could be defined more accurately as an aspiration rather a right. Non-discrimination legislation, such as the laws against discrimination (LAD), makes specific conduct an offence when it relates to certain categories of status. Being mistreated or discriminated against on the basis of age falls under this legislation, and redress can be sought under the appropriate acts. The World Health

Organisation issues a report on violence and health in 2002, stating that elderly abuse has started to be recognised as a serious problem. The WHO report highlighted the fact that a better knowledge of elder abuse was a priority worldwide and more standards were needed in scientific research on elder abuse.[14]

Power to the Elderly

Today, the elderly community lead longer, healthier, and more productive lives than ever before and are showing the strength of their mettle and what silver power can achieve. They have started to unite and recalibrate the attitudes of the public and officials toward the elderly population. Reaching the age of pension entitlement was traditionally seen as a *millstone* that brought infirmity and frailty rather than a *milestone* that signified a new beginning. Technology today provides many improvements to the quality of life of the elderly. Mobile phones and Skype have allowed communication to extend beyond the immediate walls and across continents. Alarm systems, CCTV cameras, and panic buttons provide security and protection against intruders. Life expectancy has increased by decades, and elderly people have started to lead busy, productive, and adventurous retirement lives. Now one of the fastest growing sectors in society, commercial companies have responded by investing research and technology into finding solutions to problems associated with ageing. In the last decade, significant developments have been made to improve or remove traditional difficulties associated with hearing, vision, dental, and other traditional constraints.

Stereotyping that promoted a culture of elder abuse is fast becoming blatantly outdated and misleading. Older people know how to live. After all, they have been doing it longer than those who govern and their wisdom should never be underestimated. Across the globe, governments become slower to introduce cost-cutting measures into budgets for the elderly, as they are the first to calibrate the effect on their lives. They are a deeply politicised community and keenly follow matters of public and political concern. They are exceptionally well informed and are the group most likely to vote. They know how the system works, and they don't get fooled easily. They have never had the support they needed in the past but have begun to show the collective power of their political acumen by ensuring optimum coverage on national news. They have learnt to kick up a stink and show that their vulnerability can be used as clout to increase attention and garner sympathy rather than be used as a target for abuse.

The population division of the United Nations has predicted that the number of people aged sixty or over is expected to nearly triple from 673 million in 2005 to two billion in 2050. The population "aged eighty or over is growing faster than any other segment of the population. Globally, the number of eighty year olds will likely increase more than fourfold from eighty-eight million in 2005 to 402 million in 2050."[15] Eurostat predicts that within the European Union the number of people aged sixty-five years or over is expected to increase in number from 84.6 million in 2008 to 151.5 million in 2060. Similarly, the number of people aged eighty or over in the EU is projected to almost triple from 21.8 million in 2008 to 61.4 million in 2060.[16]

As the elderly community unites, it proves to be a viable force. This community, once synonymous with being isolated, at risk of being forgotten, and suffering from granny burnout, has started to pool resources and intelligence, and become a force de résistance, by forming communities and committees at national and international levels.

Elderly people today are often fitter, richer, and stronger than their antecedents and are able to enjoy happy and active lives long into their retirement. They have much more to live for than many half their age and serve to highlight the formidable force that is silver power. Associating in greater numbers than ever before, people in their golden years are formulating aspirations into legislation and creating a new chapter for older people that will hopefully be realised and benefited by successive generations.

If we design for the young, we exclude the old: but if we design for the old, we include the young.

Chapter 12 ❧
Institutional Bullying

Bullying behaviour operates at any level where dominance and power causes harm, deprivation, or injury to a weaker party. Lost in presumptions of entitlement and power, establishments can lose sight of their function to serve citizens and operate practices that are oppressive, exploitative, over controlling and seed abusive behaviour. Trapped within vast metastasised institutional systems with few escapes, citizens can be choked by the institutional noose of authority and dominance that tightens around their lives. If the word demagogue had not been coined by the ancient Greeks, it would probably have been invented to define the patronage, excesses, and autonomy of institutions.[1]

Good governance is defined by the United Nations "as processes' and institutions that produce results that meet the needs of society."[2] Institutions can also be described as organisations that provide services to citizens but are not subject to the normal challenges of competence under consumer legislation to test whether they provide necessary and quality services to citizens. Institutions can also be described as organisations run by officials where the level of corruption in office must be measured annually by Transparency International (TI). TI formulates an official index of corruption in 176 countries on the perception of corruption conducted by officials on a scale of 100 to 0, where 100 is clean and 0 is highly corrupt. The annual Corruption Perception Index (CPI),[3] which repeatedly measures high levels of corruption, hardly signals an acceptance by citizens that institutions are meeting the needs of society but rather an outcry that demands change.

Rule through Dominance

Oligarchs, emperors, despots, dictators, dynasties, monarchs, and ascendancies were the traditional ruling-class models that operated across the globe for centuries. The principles of rule were based on the ruling class, taking dominant positions of hierarchical supremacy, which often amounted to tyrannical or at best unequal relationships with citizens. The doyens of power amassed great personal control and wealth, while the *hoi polloi* adopted the role of civil obedience, servility, and dutiful compliance. Authorities were genuflected to with a blind, unquestioning reverence, and those outside economic and social influence had few or no rights. Citizens were discouraged from speaking out against the ruling class, and those found questioning their authority could be found guilty of treason, which was punishable by hanging. Power differentials of dominance and submission also extended to churches and institutions as a way to repress the majority and maintain the ascendancy of the privileged few. For centuries, financial, social, and political differentials were accepted as the norm, until enlightenment, reformation, and revolutionary battles transformed and shifted the balance of power. In the aftermath of dynasties, despots, and dictators power differentials were considered to be bridged and the principles of *all* people having an equal say were committed to declarations, bills, and constitutions that became the founding principles of democracy.

A Breach of Trust

Few democrats today, however, can cheer about the level of

control that they have in shaping their own lives, influence how their communities develop, or change how their countries are managed. Political systems have become re-established into state institutions and organisations with hierarchical systems of control, and thrones to place a few individuals who have secured formal dominant and unrestrained positions of power. On many levels, the old culture of absolute power and dominance has slowly resurfaced and may only have transferred from the old regimes of absolute rule to a handful of representatives in the new establishments.

Senior officials, who are legitimately entrusted with unlimited power and budgets, rack up unrealistic pay hikes and privileges with little or no accountability. No legislation, penalisations, or policies regulate the behaviour of officials who can become blinkered, corrupt, out of control, and dictatorial. Captaining the future course of many nations, state-owned establishments are plunged into losses by officials whose actions, decisions, and positions of stewardship have become untouchable. Corruption by officials, which includes nepotism, bribery, and embezzlement, are absorbed into the national culture, providing a national role model of a brutal system of corruption that legitimises the abuse of power in positions of trust. The CPI index highlights an acceptance of behaviour on a systems level that supports the practice of wrongdoing to others. The index provides evidence of the gateway of abuse that is open to people in positions of trust. The index reflects the established *modus operandi* in official office, which allows unprecedented levels of autonomy and allows a flood of corrupt behaviour to permeate. In 1999, Pepler and Craig defined bullying as "negative actions which may be physical or verbal, have hostile intent, are repeated over time, and involve a power differential."[4] This definition aptly describes how corrupt behaviour in public office transfers to consequences for citizens, such as tax cuts, personal debt, and negative equity. Livelihoods get thrown off course, and distress, anxiety, and misery are created in the lives of citizens for decades. Democratic principles attacked and debased by the hierarchical donors to the process who abuse their positions, place the system itself under attack. All over the globe, unrestrained power by officials in high office became predatory and vast.[5] This behaviour adds testimony to the fact that abuse of trust and corruption will generally follow when huge differentials of power and vulnerability are established.

The state and its officials play many pivotal roles in modelling and shaping standards that become a blueprint for public behaviour. As legislators they define the limits of tolerable behaviour and acceptable conduct within society from which standards of behaviour accordingly follow. The actions of officials also act as a filter to interpret expected maxims of behaviour and values. In official office corruption sanctions values of disrespect, illicit conduct, and irresponsibility. Abuse of trust becomes systemically adopted into the subculture and the shared belief system of society. Undermining the principles of fairness and moral conduct, negative conditions and practices in and of themselves create a culture of bullying and harassment. Over time, the establishment itself is perceived as operating double standards and holding negative attitudes.

A Systems Failure
Consumer rights provide a system of redress to ensure that standards must apply to goods and services that are provided in the

course of a business. Citizens experiencing unsatisfactory services and indifference from government departments and established organisations, such as banks, however, must follow a separate system of complaints procedures. In many cases, complaints made are exclusively dealt with internally with no system of appeal to an authority, such as an ombudsman. In the absence of any appeal procedure or protection under consumer legislation, however, a complaint often becomes conveniently shifted onto a system where nobody is held responsible. Making written complaints can serve to be a distraction from the source of the problem rather than a solution. Serious complaints of corruption or requests for accountability, become removed from the jurisdiction of both citizens and courts, and shifted into the privileged realms of official enquiries, investigations, and tribunals.

Determinations of innocence or guilt in criminal matters, such as corruption, which are solely a matter for the courts, are handed over to tribunals, enquiries, and investigations. With no power to prosecute, these systems of redress amount to toothless, costly, and long drawn-out procedures. Three silent monkeys turn into one big gorilla in a process designed by official legislators to investigate official institutions, often amounting to nothing more than official shields for corruption to hide behind. Painstaking investigations result in lengthy reports with explanations that equate to how jelly was nailed to the wall. Simply put, the conduct of public officials considered to stand *legibus solitus,* or above the law, becomes exactly that. These anomalies ensure the practices of dominance and power at senior levels in official office become institutionally protected. Citizens witnessing the wrongdoings of senior officials, followed by a costly system of redress that protects these wrongdoings can have far-reaching effects on the overall culture of society. If allowed to continue unchecked, a state of unrestrained deep-rooted political corruption, called kleptocracy can result. According to the *Merriam-Webster Dictionary,* kleptocracy is "government by those who seek chiefly status and personal gain at the expense of the governed."[6] Anti-bullying policies have not been strengthened to challenge behaviour that becomes autonomous and corrupt. Eventually, people depending on the integrity of people in positions of authority become subservient to a dominating influence rather than being facilitated through a democratic function.

Thomas Hobbes, a seventeenth-century philosopher, wrote that beneath the outward veneer of civilisation, "the life of man was solitary, poor, nasty, brutish, and short."[7] Philosophers and religions have always emphasised the need for moral codes of conduct to define human interactions. Ethical principles attached to most occupational groups have evolved to avoid inflicting harm on others, and democratic governance was founded on the principle of treating all people with respect. In many countries, however, the fundamental right to dignity and respect and protection from unwanted conduct remains enshrined, confined, and buried in the lofty articles of constitutions and declarations. This inability to access rights, can amount to rights becoming aspirations rather than practical tools needed to deal with the realities of bullying that face citizens daily.

Differentials between state and citizens become more amplified when power is uploaded away from local communities and decisions are centralised to national levels. European and global unions further upload and centralise power away from individual countries. Eventually, the power to influence decisions moves further away from individuals, communities, and countries and into the less accountable realms of the political stratosphere. Democracy, once defined as rule by the people, becomes a distant, alienated, faceless, and fragile model of international democracy where a handful of world leaders make decisions for a global population of billions. Centralising power sucks the democratic vitality from people and removes their ability to influence decisions that affect their daily lives and families. For some, this process raises huge questions on the mechanics of twenty-first-century democracy and begs the question of how people central and inclusive to democracy have become so removed and excluded from the process. Politicians, who are democratically elected to reflect the mandate of the people, often owe their allegiance to the whip or the central cabinet of government above them. Left with no constitutional existence of their own, politicians without a mandate serve to weaken the purpose and integrity of the democratic union, as citizens become reduced to little more than bystanders.

Institutions that shift responsibility onto a system that fails to hold anybody accountable make contradictions at the heart of society more apparent. It exposes larger questions, such as how institutions set up to serve citizens, diffuse responsibility, and develop their own rules and standards to become moral universes of their own. Institutional dominance becomes clearly demonstrated when wrongdoings are covered up regardless of the seriousness of the mistakes made. Members of the establishment bond and unite in the shared conviction that the establishment must be protected. Using the rationale that is typical of mobbing behaviour, scandals and mistakes made by churches, banks, and state institutions are covered-up. This is done in the skewed belief that the credibility attached to the office must be protected against what is perceived as an attack on the establishment. A collective collusion builds, placing the interests of the establishment firmly above any wrongdoing to the individual. Responsibility given by the state to protect citizens is abjured in favor of protecting the reputation and authority of the institution. Misplaced loyalties and values betray human dignity, and the rights of citizens become disregarded through the democratic process. On many levels the establishments can act to strengthen or weaken the position of citizens. Hiding behind title, status, rank, profession and authority, officials sit on the institutional throne of indifference. Like turning the key in a car whose battery refuses to ignite, attempts by citizens to question their actions are met with layers of procedures and deadlines that act as barriers to complaints. Making it financially punitive to mount a challenge, institutions engage legal attack armies or introduce privileged systems of redress to defend their position. This defence ultimately contributes to a culture and climate of institutional power and control, and a weakening of the position of citizens in the union. Liefooghe and Davey explored organisational and institutional power systems and found evidence for concern.[8]

Corporate Bullying
Company formations operate as separate third-party legal entities under corporate statutes. Profits, which are often greater than the GDP of many countries, place corporations into powerful positions of political and economic influence. Sweeping across the globe in search of competitive pickings, superpowers can grow into gargantuan size and amass enormous profits. Like any entity of power and strength, this can be used to expand and grow in the wonderful, competitive playground of business and enterprise. Positions can also be used to transcend legal jurisdictions and take advantage of circumstances in which people have few rights. In the wake of Enron, WorldCom, and other publicised scandals more attention has been paid to business ethics. These scandals highlighted the harmful impact that corporate behaviour can have on people's lives, which caused a general outcry for higher standards of conduct in businesses.

Protecting Citizens against Corruption
Since 2003, the United Nations designated December 9 as the UN International Anti-corruption Day to heighten awareness on

corruption.[9] This day is dedicated to "cracking down on corruption, shaming those who practice it and engendering a culture that values ethical behaviour." Nurses, solicitors, psychologists, and other professionals are required to hold membership with professional bodies that oversee standards and investigate complaints. State officials, however, once in positions of power, leave citizens with very few options to question or shame them.

Put the Whistle Down—Someone Might Hear You.

The UN Convention against Corruption (UNCAC),[10] adopted in 2005, and previous EU Council of Europe Conventions on Criminal and Civil Corruption acknowledge that corruption and economic crimes are committed by officials at national levels. In most cases, however, anti-corruption legislation provides few solutions on any practical level to allow citizens raise issues. Solutions have resulted in a process of investigation that presents taxpayers with costs that amount to millions, and has provoked huge debate about lengthy trials and expert objective evidence that brings any satisfactory solutions.

Twenty-one Ways to Skin Whistleblowers
Highly paid senior officials are the favourite contenders to ensure that anti-corruption standards and practices apply at institutional levels. However, bystanders have been chosen to report the shortcomings of institutions through whistle blowing legislation.

According to the *Merriam-Webster Dictionary*, the definition of underdog is defined as a person having "the least odds of influencing a change in practice in a struggle or contest."[11] Whistleblowers would generally fit this position as they are open to reprisals, such as suspensions, termination of employment, bullying, legal claims of libel, and false allegations. Nevertheless, they are called upon to blow the whistle and expose the dishonest, incompetent, and corrupt operation of institutions that by their own standards, find nothing wrong with their practices. Mayhew and McCarthy argued that statutes to protect whistleblowers needed to be strengthened to safeguard against the use of bullying, which allowed corruption to persist.[12] Nevertheless, anti-bullying legislation has not been strengthened. Systems to highlight, detect, or restrain corrupt activity at institutional levels have not been introduced. Strict penalisations to act as deterrents to committing corrupt crimes in official office are not in place. Consumer rights to allow citizen's test the competency of institutional services do not apply. Civil actions allowing citizens compensation for corrupt activity in official office are not in place, and practical systems to investigate corruption in official office are not in operation.

Placing responsibility on whistleblowers suggests that, if nobody blows the whistle, no problems exist. If problems are found retrospectively, the blame may conveniently fall on individuals who had the option to blow the whistle but did not. In May 2013, a doctor "blew the whistle" on the National Health Service in the UK. The doctor was reported as being bullied, mentally ill, falsely accused of being abusive, and then suspended. It was later reported on the Chanel 4 news that the doctor said there were "twenty-one ways to skin a whistleblower."[13]

Following from any investigation, officials, with the sanctuary of continued salaries and pensions may only incur a disciplinary procedure. Whistleblowers, however, may become scapegoats for the inefficiencies of senior officials, be bullied, suspended, and become selfless martyrs by ruining their chances of promotion, and effectively blowing the lid on their own careers.

Chapter 13 ～

The Price of Negative Psychosocial Behaviour

The financial cost of mistreating people may seem a cold place to estimate a loss when you add up the tragedies of victims and families whose lives have been ruined through the behaviour of bullying. However, in the devastating, silent aftermath that is created, a powerful catalyst is lost for changing the behaviour if nothing is done to quantify the financial losses.

To date, the costs of negative psychosocial behaviour in the workplace, cyber community, or school community are not calculated as a cost to these organisations or to society in general. A study was commissioned by the International Labour Organisation (ILO) in the late nineties to estimate the cost of violence and stress in the workplace. The research was undertaken by the Manchester University Technical Institute of Science and Technology, which published its findings in 2001. In its study, entitled *The cost of Violence/Stress at Work and the Benefits of a Violence/Stress Free Working Environment,* the institute reported that the total cost of stress and violence at work as being between 1 to 3.5 percent of GDP.[1] In Germany in 1999, the over-all damage of workplace bullying was rated at between €15 and €50 billion per year.[2] These findings suggest that the cost of negative psychosocial behaviour is a significant financial problem, compromising individuals and organisations and exponentially placing a substantial financial burden on society. The ILO study on *The Cost of Violence/Stress at Work and the Benefits of a Violence/Stress Free Working Environment*, however, was not updated nor was it extended to estimate the cost of negative psychosocial behaviour in schools, elderly care units, the Internet, and other communities. If these multiple and massive costs were included, the total costs would probably represent a shockingly larger percentage of GDP—way beyond the upper range of 3.5 percent estimated for the workplace alone.

With no monitoring systems in place to quantify the costs of negative psychosocial behaviour, scant information is available to governments, policy makers, unions, and the public to determine what changes are needed to offset these costs. This facilitates institutions and commercial organisations benefiting financially from providing services with no reciprocal duty to ensure employees are provided with safe and healthy psychosocial environments to work in. It also allows an undetermined and unproductive financial drain to be placed on society, which contributes substantially to national exchequer debt.

Calculating the Cost

In the workplace, the behaviour of bullying can inhibit or reduce the delivery of excellence and quality in the provision of goods and services. It can discourage investment and collectively affect the capacity of enterprises to maintain profitability. In schools, bullying reduces the quality of learning and the ability of students to perform in exams. In the cyber community, which is the new social interactive environment for children and adults, the models of behaviour and interaction have pushed out the boundaries of treating people with disrespect and cruelty and allowed the behaviour of bullying to accelerate and become prescriptively built into all communities with a corresponding drain on social support services and an associated escalation in costs.

In this chapter, models to estimate the costs of bullying behaviour are taken from the workplace, but these can be successfully adopted and transferred to estimate the costs in other communities, such as schools, elderly care units, and the cyber community. The model used in this exercise is based on the study completed by Hoel, Sparks, and Cooper commissioned by the ILO, entitled *Cost of Violence/Stress at Work and the Benefits of a Violence/Stress-Free Working Environment*. The study completed in 2001 gave recognition to the comprehensive costs that are generated as a result of bullying behaviour. The study demonstrates that costs are not just confined to the losses borne by individuals but are extended to organisations and the state, which together form the combined aggregate cost to society as a whole.[3]

The Cost of Bullying to Organisations

Factors considered when estimating the cost to organisations include staff turnover, absenteeism, and sick leave, including the associated costs of cover and replacement. A typical case of workplace bullying in Britain was estimated in 2003 as costing the organisation £28,109.[4] In the United States, the estimated cost of an average individual incident of bullying was found to be $25,000, and the total cost to American employers nationally per year was estimated at $4.2 billion.[5] A financial calculation based on a model by Monica Henderson in Australia estimated that individual cases of bullying cost the employer $16,977, and the total national cost to Australian employers was between $6 and $13 billion each year.[6]

Cost of Absenteeism

A report, published by the European Parliament entitled "Bullying at Work," stated that one of the consequences from workplace bullying was an increase in absenteeism. The report found that 34 percent of workers exposed to bullying were absent from work, compared with an average 23 percent among workers in general.[7] A study of two Finnish hospital districts found staff who were bullied had a 26 percent greater medically certified absence rate than staff who were not bullied.[8]

In the workplace, staff can account for between 50 to 80 percent of the total cost of overheads. Loss of time through premature retirement, constructive dismissal, staff turnover, replacement, absenteeism, and sick leave can, therefore, have a substantial effect on productivity and profit. The general requirements from Occupational Health and Safety authorities (OHS) in most countries, including the EU Directive 89/391/EEC, requires employers to record "occupational" illnesses from employees absent from work for more than three working days.[9] As psychosocial illnesses associated with workplace bullying behaviour are not officially defined as "occupational," no statutory obligations exist to notify authorities of these absences. Statistics on bullying are not published on annual occupational health and safety summary reports, and absences resulting from bullying behaviour cannot be calculated nationally. To quantify the cost of absenteeism as a result of workplace bullying in the UK, a study was commissioned, which estimated that forty million working days a year were lost through stress-related illness. It was further estimated that one-third to one-half of these illnesses may have been as a result of workplace bullying.[10]

Failure to have a system in place to financially quantify the cost of absences that result from bullying behaviour, leaves a gaping financial hole that is haemorrhaging money. No information to quantify the problem exists, so no pressure exists to find solutions. In the private sector, absenteeism can result in companies creating overheads that cost them out of the market. In the public sector, the costs become incalculable and conveniently externalised and dumped onto taxpayers who become the involuntary donors who pay the price.

Replacement Costs
Replacement costs stem from expenditure linked to recruitment, selection, and training. This can include short periods of cover

for sickness and absenteeism or full replacement costs due to staff turnover. The UK's trade union UNISON found that bullying significantly affected turnover rates, reporting that 26.4 percent of those bullied said they left their jobs due to bullying.[11] Replacement costs include interviewing, advertising, testing, checking references, and issuing new contracts. Also affecting the cost of replacement is the reduced capacity of new recruits following initial start-up. Based on the study by Gordon and Risley, Hoel, Sparks, and Cooper set the average replacement costs of employees at approximately £1,900. Using the prevalent rate of bullying at the time, which was 10 percent, and the rate at which people left their jobs as a result of bullying, which was approximately 25 percent, a conservative estimate was made to calculate the total cost involved in replacing staff, which was calculated as being in the order of £380 million.[12]

Presenteeism

This term refers to individuals who remain present at work after being bullied with reduced morale and performance capacity. Estimating the cost of downtime and unproductive time is difficult, as the effects of bullying can be traumatic and far-reaching. The behaviour is linked to tension and anxiety, which leads to reduced motivation and concentration. The residual negative atmosphere and low staff morale can result in employees being unable to carry out normal work, particularly whilst incidents are ongoing or investigations are being conducted. The behaviour leads to impaired performance, decreased output, and reduced standards as well as additional errors, mistakes, and accidents. The study completed by Hoel, Sparks, and Cooper estimated that staff who were bullied had an overall drop in productivity rates of approximately 7 percent.[13] According to their report, indirect exposure to bullying also affected individuals negatively by inducing fear and tension to those in close proximity who witnessed co-workers being victimised.[14]

Grievance and Complaints

The early resolution of complaints is of great importance, as costs associated with tensions remain high until an outcome is reached. Costs are more likely to increase if the situation is allowed to fester and trigger extremes in behaviour. Escalation of the behaviour is likely to incur the use of industrial relations procedures with additional outlay in costs for absenteeism and downtime for employees to attend hearings.

Legal and Medical Costs to Organisations

Legal and medical representatives become some of the main beneficiaries from bullying and harassment in the workplace. Lengthy periods of legal wrangling, which appears to be a growing tendency in bullying cases,[15] has resulted in medical and legal professionals carving out lucrative careers in the pursuit of litigation battles. Employee medical costs must be paid by employers, if treatment plans are included under employment contracts. National agreements may require employers to provide counselling services to targets and perpetrators that follow from incidents of bullying. Legal battles call on doctors, consultants, therapists, and specialists from both sides to provide reports and expert professional opinions in an effort to gain a legal advantage. Days lost from work through mediation, medical appointments, and court hearings for witnesses, victims, and management must be paid by employers. Intangible costs may arise through publicity that prompts negative images of the company, a drop in sales and employee morale. Legal remedies finally delivered may not provide solutions, as the problems often remain in the system waiting to reoccur.

Insurance Costs for Organisations

These costs are often overlooked, but insurance companies can provide generous protection to challenges made to large organisations and institutions. A legal attack army can offer financial immunity to senior officials in public institutions and senior managers in private industry, which is often the key factor deciding that mistakes made at the top stay at the top. Employees, in sharp polarised conflict with managers can be faced with insurance policies that offer legal cover to senior management, in the event of a claim being brought. As a result of mounting disputes and legal challenges, companies and institutions can find getting reinsured difficult.[16] Organisations may have to pay increased hikes in premiums when renewing their policies.

The Cost of Bullying for Individuals

The model used to calculate the cost for organisations are often the same as those incurred by individuals, except they are computed differently. Escape strategies used by employees to cope with bullying behaviour at work, such as absenteeism, reduced hours, and sickness are calculated as the difference between normal earnings and what is received when absent from work or working in a reduced capacity. In cases where individuals feel they have to leave their jobs, careers may be lost or have to be re-built and new qualifications acquired. The typical health consequences from bullying and abusive treatment are heart attacks, ulcers, psoriasis, anxiety, post-traumatic stress disorder, migraines, and depression. These can be accompanied by depression, sleep difficulties, anxiety, drug and alcohol dependency, and suicide ideation. Although these conditions are not life threatening, they may last indefinitely and require constant personal medical maintenance and management.

Legal and Medical Costs to Individuals

Costs borne by individuals include personal medical bills and a range of care treatments. These treatments can result in health insurance costs rising, which in some cases can amount to a 50 percent increase.[17] Investigation and litigation costs are incurred, together with travel and accommodation costs, if court jurisdictions are outside the area of residence. Legal claims must be supported by reports from expert and specialist professionals, and evidence may be required to be given in court.

Additional Human Costs

As comprehensive studies identify the interconnectedness between bullying behaviour and the severe traumatic impact of bullying on victims,[18] distinctions are made between "financial costs" and "human costs." Human costs are associated with pain, fear, stress, health, and "a general reduction in the overall quality of life." Human suffering can take over the lives of people who have been traumatically affected by bullying and can no longer perform basic everyday tasks. Less than-adequate-parenting go hand in hand with the trauma of being bullied. Additional child minding, transport, and cleaning costs follow because of being emotionally and physically incapacitated. Strained relationships can develop with partners, spouses, friends, neighbours, and relatives, which can culminate in out-of-control teenagers, a breakdown in marriages, friendships, and a loss of custody arrangement with children. Reduced concentration and motivation over prolonged periods of time can negatively affect the ability of employees to work productively and student's to perform in their studies and exams. The trauma and snowballing effect created can result in the loss of a job, career, exams, home, relationships, health, well-being, and sometimes even life.

The Cost to Governments

The long-term effects of bullying behaviour are ultimately paid by the state. The state picks up the tab for unemployment benefits if people leave their jobs. National insurance schemes pay claims to employees who suffer injuries in the workplace. National schemes under Employee Assisted Programmes (EAP) provide counselling to parties affected by the behaviour, which is funded in public office by the state. The state provides the cost of industrial relations, labour relations, and other state mediation and investigation services required to resolve disputes. Criminal investigations, prosecutions, and imprisonment are paid by the state. The cost of absenteeism and replacement of staff in public offices are also borne by the state. In Scotland, teachers suffering from stress in 2003 were estimated to cost the taxpayer a staggering £43 million with a further £37 million paid for supply teachers to cover those "off sick."[19] Insurance hikes for schools, colleges, and public institutions are paid by the state as well as legal expenses. In Germany, in 1999, the overall cost of workplace bullying was estimated as being between €15 and €50 billion per year.[20]

Failing to Monitor and Quantify the Problem

With high financial burdens placed on taxpayers, questions arise relating to the financial cost of bullying to society, like; why policy makers allow costs to become externalised to society, like; why public and private enterprises do not have a "defined duty of care" with responsibility for ensuring that people are protected against negative psychosocial risks when in their care; why national monitoring systems are not in place to quantify the cost of absenteeism due to bullying behaviour; or why the total cost of the behaviour to society is not quantified. Failing to monitor how people are treated in society leads to a gradual numbing of human response and a collective detachment or unconscious drift away from social cohesion. While the financial cost of bullying behaviour is estimated through studies and surveys, the human price often remains incalculable.

The study commissioned by the ILO conducted by Hoel, Sparks, and Cooper in 2001 showed that costs from one-on-one violence extends into organisations and becomes externalised as a cost to society. In 2005 these studies were updated by Chappell and Di Martino, again showing that the ripple effect of violence is distributed outward into society.[21] Primary intervention involves the introduction of regulations to prevent and manage risks that relate to unwanted conduct. Secondary intervention focuses on improving the individual's ability to cope and manage work stresses and workloads through training. Tertiary intervention focuses on rehabilitating the parties that suffer from stress through support systems and intervention, which involves the highest cost to society. Despite the numerous studies showing the correlates between bullying behaviour and the costs incurred for absenteeism, replacement costs, reduced productivity, insurance, and increased staff turnover, the chosen solution to resolving negative psychosocial behaviour continues to be an increase in management time and expertise after incidents occur. No mandatory alternatives have been introduced by most countries to invest in a fraction of these costs to introduce primary or secondary intervention. Tertiary intervention remains the most popular option, which is the most expensive, and involves the highest costs to society. It also provides an instant and cost-effective solution to lazy and incompetent organisations through the externalisation or dumping of the majority of the costs onto society and the taxpayers.

Fraud and Crime

When people are mistreated, the effect of the behaviour is externalised and attached to human value. Many correlates have been identified between people being unfairly treated and counter-productive behaviour, such as vandalism, sabotage, and fraud. Victims linked to powerlessness with little control over their lives commonly use fraud and violence as an outlet for frustration. In schools that were attacked by shooters, investigations later reported that, in some cases, the attackers had experienced bullying and harassment in the school, and that "the experience of bullying appeared to play a major role in motivating the attack on the school."[22]

Globalising the Costs of Bullying

The financial arm of the United Nations, the International Monetary Fund (IMF), identified four aspects to globalization in 2000. These were trade, capital movements, the movement of people, and the spread of knowledge (and technology).[23] In the global integration of billions of people from diverse economic, religious, ethnic, and cultural backgrounds, the human integration of people is not identified as being a significant aspect of globalisation. Integration is almost exclusively referred to in terms of world trade and financial markets, where the main players are companies and countries that buy and sell. Not including psychosocial integration, as being as important as other aspects of globalization, such as financial and trading integration, has created barriers for many people ever realising the global dream. In the bigger financial global game of monopoly, the way people are treated is not factored into the rules. The costs of ignoring this problem is not calculated by the IMF or by the Organisation for Economic Cooperation and Development (OECD)[24] or any international or national organisation or union that the author could find. In framing global policy today, people could not be blamed for believing they have started to come last. The opportunity to introduce international rules and regulations at primary and secondary levels to assist and steer the human global integration process is lost. At best, human illnesses that result from negative psychosocial behaviour are treated as a by-product or collateral fall-out from trade and financial activity.

It's Dog eat Dog Out There!

No investment, focus, or regulations are put in place to ensure that international standards of behaviour are applied in communal areas of activity, such as schools, the workplace or Internet. This omission perpetuates the lowering of conditions and standards of behaviour between people. In an effort to strike a competitive edge in the tendering process, pressure continues to be loaded onto employees, who experience increased demands and increased levels of stress. The vulnerability of employees is heightened, and the risk of one-on-one violence increases. Without international regulations for human integration among diverse communities that engage in cost competitions, an escalation in negative behaviour becomes inevitable. The costly aftermath unavoidably becomes randomly dispersed and debited to countries and communities, resulting in the global integration and resolution of costly behavioural problems but not the profits.

Chapter 14 ∾
The Role of Trade Unions

Citizens throughout the world who were failed by governments and political leaders often looked to unions as the only vehicle to protect and establish their rights as workers. Trade unions became the vital component of society through which employees aspired to greater justice, equality, and welfare at work.

Being a member of a trade union became illegal in many countries and punishments, including executions, were often given for attempting to organise one. Union membership in some countries, such as Columbia, continued to be dangerous, with a total of twenty-nine people murdered in 2011 for their trade union activity.[1] Despite these obstacles, the union movement has grown in size, not only legalising membership but also codifying the relationship between employers and employees. Today, unions represent millions of members across the globe and form partnerships with employer groups and governments through participation in tripartite negotiations both at national and international levels. From the late 1800s, unions began to acquire political power and influence and became affiliated to national trade union centres, which were generally called federations, confederations, or congresses. National trade union centres formed by trade unions became the established national representative bodies that negotiated collective agreements on wages at national levels with employer and government representatives. National trade union centres, in turn, became affiliated to European and international trade union organisations.

Union Size and Revenue

Through their growth, organisation, and success, unions have established themselves as the collective voice of working people in most countries. Amongst the largest national trade union centres in the world are the All-China Federation of Trade Unions (ACFTU), which is the nationalised worker organisation federation of the People's Republic of China with 134 million workers. The largest national trade unions in the United States are the American Federation of Labor and the Congress of Industrial Organisations (AFL-CIO) and the Change to Win Federation (CTW). In Canada, the Canadian Labour Congress (CLC) is the largest. The European Trade Union Confederation (ETUC) is the representative trade union of EU member states. In Ireland, the Irish Trade Union Congress (ITUC) is the largest. In Britain, the Trade Union Congress (TUC) is the predominant national trade union centre. The Australian Council of Trade Unions (ACTU) is the largest centre in Australia. The world's largest international representative union is the International Trade Union Confederation (ITUC). In 2013, the official website of ITUC noted that it represented 175 million workers through 315 national affiliated trade union organisation centres within 156 countries or territories around the world.[2]

Trade union membership is measured as a percentage of the working population, which is referred to as union density ratings. Membership varies considerably between countries with union density: in Finland, rating at about 90 percent, while Estonia and Lithuania are below 10 percent.[3] Union membership figures can be estimated roughly from the total number of people employed nationally and the national union density rating figures for that country. Using the total membership figures, the total national revenue for unions can be estimated using the union membership figures and the average annual cost for union fees.

In 2008, the European Foundation reported that unions across Europe represented a little over fifty-eight million workers.[4] Union members paying an average membership fee of €100 per year may generate revenue from the total European Union membership of approximately €5.8 billion. If the collective international ITUC membership of 175 million members were taken as paying an annual membership of €100, a staggering total of €17.5 billion would be estimated annually from the international union membership. Unions are generally awarded non-profit organisation (NPO) status, which allows non-taxable surplus revenue to be retained and reinvested for the self-preservation of the union's principals, growth, and expansion.

Social Partnerships

The operational mechanism for most unions from 1987 up to the financial stalemate in 2009 was through social partnership, where unions enjoyed unprecedented political and economic influence. During the period 1987 to 2009, tripartite agreements were reached in most countries between government officials, the main employer groups, and the unions. At EU level, European Social Partners engage in reaching framework agreements, which can remain as agreements or adopted to be given EU directive status by the European Council.

Collective agreements negotiated at national levels between the social partners are commonly known as "soft arrangements." Their success is totally dependent on the effectiveness and influence of the unions to deliver these agreements to their membership. In the absence of legislation, they provide solid guidelines and precursors to finding solutions, and many examples of non-regulatory instruments work well. However, agreements can lose their focus and strength when they purport to be a substitute for legislation. This is especially the case when employees are increasingly subject to demands and pressures that are out of keeping with their abilities, skills, and coping strategies. In the absence of legislation, employees with increased work demands can find it impossible to find any basis to protect or counteract the overloads being applied.

Corporate Agreements

There are many good examples of corporate agreements that have been reached between companies and employees, which have become increasingly popular. In Germany, an agreement reached with Volkswagen in 1996 was aimed at establishing an enterprise culture. Employees formed committees and councils with management to deal with various aspects of employee welfare and company enterprise. Agreements in place facilitate intervention when problems arise and appropriate action becomes effective immediately.

Profit before People

Despite considerable revenue and a vast international union membership base, stark variations in international standards for workers continue. Standards of quality and excellence apply universally to commodities and services across all countries. However, a lack of harmonisation in standards and conditions for workers facilitates the downward spiral of rights owed to employees in an effort to increase cost competition. No international agreements apply to workers, even in countries with trading agreements and universal affiliations. Disproportionate variations in international working conditions create increased competition. No restrictions apply to countries that trade internationally with reduced standards to workers, and no penalties apply to countries or companies that violate international human rights agreements. This situation sustains a short-sighted approach to countries being tempted to create jobs at any cost. Ultimately, it pits countries against each other in competitions to win investment and trade contracts by placing economic performance ahead of people. A cost advantage is allowed to countries that provide reduced standards and conditions to workers, while countries providing standards and supports are penalised financially. In a competition of profit and loss, labour becomes calculated in the same way as other stock commodities. Profits are credited to countries that win investment and trade contracts, while losses are debited to countries that pay multiple medical and social supports schemes to workers.

Some unions make huge contributions at national and international levels by sensitising governments to the changing needs of their members and conducting surveys to raise awareness of the rapidly changing pressures their members are experiencing. Other unions conduct no surveys, make little or no measurable representation to governments, and make few, if any, challenges to courts on behalf of members. Many believe that some unions have become absorbed into another arm of the state, primarily reinvesting in their own salaries and abrogating their responsibilities to their members. Accepting industrial relations procedures and legislation on behalf of members that is not fit for purpose exposes some unions as paying little more than lip service to the genuine concerns of members who are over stretched, over stressed, and under pressure. This acceptance betrays the trust placed in unions by members who seek safeguards to protect their health while sustaining a livelihood. Commitment and loyalty given by workers is not reciprocated by employers and unions to ensure that preventative measures against psychosocial trauma are implemented in the workplace.

The days when trade union leaders with outstretched hands gave inspirational speeches to get people to stand up and march for their rights are gone. Today, standing up is more about giving people the legal rights that they need to stop the global productivity squeeze and put people before profit or at least be placed on an equal standing. Some unions with the traditional task of executing industrial action and showing solidarity with workers through strikes and pickets, appear confused about achieving newly defined aims and strategies. Unions criticise government policy, giving the impression they are disgruntled with government performance. Yet, unions are active partners participating in the process. Failing to widen their agenda, unions do little to prevent the haemorrhaging of money through the multiple losses created through violence and stress in the workplace. Acting more as observers rather than participants, unions sit on the sidelines. If they appear shy about undertaking new innovative approaches to protecting their members, unions are not participating as key donors to the process.

Critical to achieving an effective response to workers' rights at an international level is the union's participation in tripartite negotiations at the ILO conference level. Participation at this level shapes and determines the rights of workers globally through the introduction of conventions and the updating and introduction of occupational illnesses and diseases. To date, the lack of any convention to outlaw unwanted behaviour against *all* people in the workplace reflects badly on the basic principles held by trade union organisation to promote fair treatment for *all* workers. Trade unions, which fail to ensure that stress is included on the official list of occupational diseases, speaks badly of an organisation that represents greater justice for workers.

Stopping the Bullying

Governments come and go, but unions steeped in a history of workers' rights were established to ensure that the balance between the respect and value owed to workers is not compromised above financial goals. In today's competitive markets, protecting the health of workers against unwanted conduct and unrealistic demands becomes a real challenge for unions and workers.

To date, the workplace is the only community where legislation has been predominantly introduced to combat bullying behaviour. As one of the oldest cornerstones of representative democracy, unions will hopefully continue to formulate legislation to prevent bullying behaviour for their members, which can hopefully form the basis of legislation to be introduced to other communities.

Chapter 15 ～
Culture Changes and Power Shifts

The essential right of *all* people not to be mistreated is implied as fundamentally as it is accepted that *all* people have a right to be there. At the core of combating bullying behaviour is the idea that, no matter who you are or where you are from, you are entitled to respect and dignity.

How people treat one another has always been a moral, religious, and ethical issue. It is also a political and social issue, but most of all it is a human issue. To date, however, no model exists for preventing or regulating hostile behaviour in communal environments, to protect the mental and physical well-being of people, in the same way, regulations are in place to protect ecological environments from pollution. This anomaly, gives just cause to believe that the pervasive and malignant scourge of bullying has only just begun.

The fundamental duty of good governance, which is to ensure that the dignity and respect of all citizens is guaranteed, has become buried in a maze of political, social and legal bureaucracy.

Only in a handful of countries has the legal responsibility been transferred to public or private organizations to be held accountable, incur penalties, or take responsibility for providing practical levels of guardianship to people in their care. Finding solutions in most cases has resulted in children and adults having to fight legal battles after their physical and mental health has deteriorated to such an extent that they can prove a line of behaviour has been crossed. These battles must often be fought within a system where the behaviour of bullying is not defined, no specific legislation exists to address the problem, and no European or international instrument acknowledges that the problem exists.

The ability of individuals to challenge unwanted conduct as an offence when a person's dignity is violated has only been extended in a number of limited cases on specified grounds, which is outlined in a number of successive EU Directives,[1] and specific legislation from individual countries. Unwanted conduct that violates the dignity of *all* children and *all* adults has not been made an offence, even in the communal areas where people work, learn, play, and retire.

SIDEBAR

Undermining the rights owed to citizens to prevent twisted and wrong behaviour being perpetrated against them has started to become a real threat to families and individuals. This threat highlights the power and control held by systems of dominance that have had little or no shake-up in power for generations. Culture changes and power shifts are needed to offset this imbalance by unlocking the dominance held by systems and governments and transferring power to individuals so that they can challenge hostile and offensive conduct that is directed against them.

Impediments to Regulating Psychosocial Risks

1. To date, no universal definition of bullying behaviour exists, which creates impediments to formulating the reference point from which statutes and standards are defined or mitigated.

2. The absence of definition has resulted in no specified "duty of care" being extended to social media sites, schools, workplaces, and institutional environments to frame how people are treated.

3. The absence of a statutory requirement to report or record incidents of bullying provides an impediment to gathering statistics, monitoring or preventing the behaviour, predicting future tragedies, canvassing advocacy groups, or determining when urgent changes are needed in legislation. Effectively this places bullying behaviour off-the-official-radar and facilitates the covert nature of the behaviour.

4. Financial losses from violence and stress in the workplace were officially estimated by the ILO in 2001 as being up to 3.5 percent of GDP.[2] Stress, however, is omitted from the official ILO list of occupational diseases.[3] This omission means that stress-related illnesses fall outside the official notification systems. These systems are in place to identify injuries to health in the workplace and require the introduction of coherent preventative policies to reduce

their occurrence. This omission has created an impediment to reducing the cost and the occurrences of stress-related illnesses in the workplace and the causal links to the illnesses, such as bullying.

5.   The annual cost of work-related stress in the EU15 was estimated by the EU as being €20,000 million.[4] Stress and other psychosocial illnesses, however, are omitted from the official EU schedule of occupational diseases.[5] This omission means that stress-related illnesses fall outside the official EU recording and notification systems, which are the official means of identifying injuries to health at work. This omission creates an impediment to reducing the cost and occurrences of stress-related illnesses and the causal risks to the illnesses, such as bullying.

6.   Not including illnesses, such as stress on the official occupational illness list creates impediments to risk assessments being applied to psychosocial risks, such as bullying, which is acknowledged as an antecedent to stress. This omission permits behaviour to continue in the workplace that is a risk factor to stress-related illness and, in extreme cases, a risk factor to suicide.

7.   Not including stress as an occupational illness creates impediments to victims seeking compensation from the consequences of stress-related illnesses arising from their occupations.

8.   Not including stress-related illnesses as an official occupational illness omits absenteeism due to these illnesses having a statutory obligation to be notified or reported to health and safety authorities. This omission prevents statistics being gathered by health and safety authorities to quantify these absences on national summary reports.

9.   The absence of national financial estimates to determine

the cost of negative psychosocial behaviour in the workplace pushes taxpayers into paying an incalculable financial price for a problem that is haemorrhaging money with no provision for finding solutions.

10. The absence of an international benchmark or standard to rate negative psychosocial behaviour presents an impediment to providing children with ratings for "healthy schools," workers with ratings for "healthy workplaces," citizens with "healthy institutions," and communities with "healthy psychosocial practices."

11. The absence of an international convention to regulate psychosocial risks presents an impediment to children and adults protecting their health and well-being from behaviour that has been shown to be an emotional, psychological, and physiological hazard to their health and well-being.

12. The absence of an international convention to regulate psychosocial risks presents an impediment to providing a pathway to European or International appeals when behaviour is suffered by individuals at national levels or in cyber communities.

13. The absence of any international convention to regulate bullying behaviour presents an impediment to determining when unscrupulous enterprises provide incapable guardianship to citizens.

14. The absence of any international convention to regulate bullying behaviour conducted against *all* people prevents the basic right to dignity and respect outlined in the declaration of human rights, the bill of rights and committed to the constitutions of most countries being transferred to *all* citizens in *all* communities.

15. The absence of any unilateral convention to regulate psychosocial risks permits countries competing equally in international markets with unequal financial burdens in the provision of benefits and conditions to workers, resulting in the creation of unfair competition.

16. The absence of an international convention to regulate psychosocial risks presents an impediment to challenging dominant behaviour by officials in public office who gain autonomy to commit unrestrained acts of corruption, which is otherwise made difficult to challenge.

17. Providing no qualifications to people who typically witness the behaviour of bullying creates an impediment to professionals being equipped to make a diagnosis, conduct professional intervention, or make a referral.

18. The lack of international acknowledgement of bullying through conventions, charters, or treaties, encourages communities to operate in a vacuum, developing their own rules and systems to what is, essentially, the same problem experienced in all communities. A fragmented approach has mushroomed out of control and a lack of focus has prevented progress made in one country or community being transferred to another.

Effective and efficient governance, according to the United Nations, takes place when "processes' and institutions produce results that meet the needs of society while making the best use of resources at their disposal."[6] However, governance and institutions in many cases remain loaded with economic and politically driven goals that place little value on empowering citizens to protect themselves against unwanted practices and behaviour.

Removing existing impediments to ensure that capable guardianship is delivered to people in communal areas requires a seismic shift in culture to pull back to what has become the revolutionary concept of treating people with respect, dignity, and value. Publications, meetings, reports, resolutions, guidelines, codes, manuals, and agreements churned out by unions, governments, and European and international agencies on the subject of negative psychosocial behaviour amounts to little more than lip service when episodic instances of tragedies and surveys continue to report millions of people who become defenceless to stand up to the way they are mistreated in their daily lives.

Bullying weakens the purpose and integrity of all unions based on respect and dignity, casting a long shadow over what is understood to be civil society. Without international standards and conventions to protect the dignity and value of citizens, an international competitive market is created without an international conscience. This betrays the essence and worth of humanity and reflects badly on successive generations of leaders who have allowed so many people suffer from a near-total lack of investment in the respect they are owed. In thirty years time, unanswerable questions to posterity and the lack of human response may seem perplexing to a new generation of people born into an inherited form of hostile entrapment.

As bullies, victims, and bystanders increase in numbers, those in power will hopefully be mindful not just of their duty to achieve economic success, but their duty to humanity and the moral steps needed to ensure the future dignity and respect to mankind survives.

"All that is necessary for evil to triumph is that good men (and women) do nothing." Edmund Burke.

End Notes and References ∾

Introduction
1. Transparency International, *Corruption Perception Index*.
2. Hoel, Sparks, and Cooper, *Cost of Violence/Stress at Work*, 5.
3. Darley and Latané, "Bystander Intervention," 377.
4. Golding, *Lord of the Flies*.

Chapter 1. The Global Explosion of Bullies, Victims, and Bystanders
1. *Oxford English Dictionary Online*, s.v. "Bully," http://oxforddictionaries.com/definition/english /bully.
2. Quine, "Workplace Bullying in NHS," quoted in Rayner, Hoel, and Cooper, *Workplace Bullying*, 45.
3. Leymann and Gustafsson, "Mobbing at Work," quoted in the European Foundation for the Improvement of Working and Living Conditions, *Preventing Violence and Harassment*, 61.
4. Mikkelsen and Einarsen, *Basic Assumptions and symptoms of post traumatic stress* among victims of bullying at work, quoted in European Foundation for the Improvement of Working and Living Conditions, *Preventing Violence and Harassment*, 61.
5. Einarsen, Raknes, and Matthiesen, "Mobbing og personkonflikter," quoted in Rayner, Hoel, and Cooper, *Workplace Bullying*, 51.
6. Farrington, "Understanding and Preventing Bullying," 435.
7. International Labour Conference 101 Session, 312, ref 1848 http://www.ilo.org/ilc/ILCSessions/101stSession/reports/reports-submitted/WCMS_174846/lang--en/index.htm.
8. Olweus, "Recognizing Bullying."
9. O'Connell, Pepler, and Craig, "Peer Involvement in Bullying," 438.
10. Farrington, "Understanding and Preventing Bullying," 381.
11. Zimmerman et al., "Early Cognitive Stimulation," 384–88.
12. U.S. Secret Service, "Preventing School Shootings," 14.
13. Pepler and Craig, *Making a Difference in Bullying*, 5–7.
14. McCarthy and Mayhew, *Safeguarding the Organization*, 38–58.

Chapter 2. Pollution of the Psychosocial Environment

1. Trades Union Congress, "E–Bulletin," *Risks* 510, 2011.
2. Workplace Bullying Institute, "Results of the 2010 and 2007 WBI U.S. Workplace Bullying Survey."
3. U.S. Department of Education et al., *Indicators of School Crime and Safety: 2009*, VI.
4. Comijs et al., "Elder Abuse in the Community," 887.
5. Aronson, *Nobody Left to Hate*, 20.
6. Thylefors, *Syndabockar: Om utstötning och mobbning i arbetslivet* quoted in Einarsen and Mikkelsen, "*Individual Effects of Exposure to Bullying at Work*," 128.
7. Poland, Green, and Rootman, *Settings for Health Promotion*, 4.
8. Figure 1, Basic Ecological Model of Social Environment.
9. Cowie et al., "Measuring Workplace Bullying," 49.
10. Rayner, Hoel and Cooper, *Workplace Bullying: What We Know, Who is to Blame, and What Can We Do?* Quoted in Hoel, Sparks, and Cooper, *Cost of Violence/Stress at Work*, 34.
11. Economic and Social Research Institute et al., *Bullying in the Workplace: Survey Reports, 2007*, 61.
12. European Agency for Safety and Health at Work et al., *Research on Work–Related Stress*, 68.
13. CSA, "Psychological Health and Safety in the Workplace."
14. BSI, "Guidance on the Management of Psychosocial Risks in the Workplace."
15. European Foundation for the Improvement of Working and Living Conditions, *Work–Related Stress, Preventing Violence and Harassment*, 19.
16. European Foundation for the Improvement of Living and Working Conditions, *Third European Working Conditions Survey*, quoted in European Foundation for the Improvement of Working and Living Conditions, *Work–Related Stress*, 2.
17. European Agency for Safety and Health at Work, *Annual Report 2007*, 22.
18. Lorho and Hilp, "Bullying at Work," 12.
19. Hoel and Cooper, *Destructive Conflict*, quoted in Hoel, Sparks, and Cooper, *Cost of Violence/Stress at Work*, 4.

20. Thylefors, *Syndabockar: Om utstötning och mobbning i arbetslivet* quoted in Einarsen and Mikkelsen, *"Individual Effects of Exposure to Bullying at Work,"* 128.
21. Leymann and Gustafsson, "Mobbing at Work," quoted in European Foundation for the Improvement of Working and Living Conditions, *Preventing Violence and Harassment*, 61.
22. Sebastián García, "Los riesgos psicosociales y su prevención," quoted in European Foundation for the Improvement of Working and Living Conditions, *Work–Related Stress*, 19.
23. Transparency International, *Corruption Perception Index*.
24. Darley and Latané, "Bystander Intervention," 377.
25. Leymann, "Mobbing and Psychological Terror," quoted in Chappell and Di Martino, *Violence at Work*, Third Ed., 22.

Chapter 3. The Self–Defence of Bullying

1. O'Connell, Pepler, and Craig, "Peer Involvement in Bullying," 438.
2. *Merriam-Webster OnLine*, s.v. "Slave," http://www.merriam-webster.com/dictionary/slave.
3. Mayhew et al., "Measuring the Extent of Impact," 117.
4. Roosevelt, *Reader's Digest*, 84.
5. Vail, "Words that Wound," 38.
6. McCarthy and Mayhew, *Safeguarding the Organization*, 38–58.

Chapter 4. School Bullying and Cyberbullying

1. U.S. Department of Justice Office of Community Oriented Policing Services and Sampson, *"Bullying in Schools,"* no.12, 1.
2. Due et al., "Bullying and Symptoms Among School–Aged Children," 128–132.
3. Rigby, "Relationship Between Reported Health," 465–74.
4. Olweus, "Bully/Victim Problems Among School Children," quoted in Hodgins, "Taking a Health Promotion Approach," 14.
5. Hawton, "Assessment of Suicide Risk," quoted in Rayner, Hoel, and Cooper, *Workplace Bullying*, 51.
6. Farrington, "Understanding and Preventing Bullying," 435.
7. Pepler and Craig, *Making a Difference in Bullying*, 5–7.

8. Olweus, "Recognizing Bullying."

9. Child Health Promotion Research Centre, "Resources."

10. Johnson and Johnson, "Why Violence Prevention Programs Don't Work and What Does," 63–8.

11. Zimmerman et al., "Early Cognitive Stimulation," 384–88.

12. Rigby and Slee, "Australia," quoted in Verdugo, Vere, and International Labour Office, *Workplace Violence in Service Sectors*, 15.

13. Sharp and Smith, *Tackling Bullying in Your School,* quoted in Verdugo, Vere, and International Labour Office, *Workplace Violence in Service Sectors*, 15.

14. Canadian Centre for Justice Statistics, "Youth Violent Crime," quoted in Verdugo, Vere, and International Labour Office, *Workplace Violence in Service Sectors*, 15.

15. Lösel and Bliesener, "Germany," quoted in Verdugo, Vere, and International Labour Office, *Workplace Violence in Service Sectors*, 15.

16. Ortega and Mora-Merchan, "Spain," quoted in Verdugo, Vere, and International Labour Office, *Workplace Violence in Service Sectors*, 15.

17. U.S. Department of Education, Bureau of Justice Assistance, and Shaw, *Promoting Safety in Schools*, quoted in Verdugo, Vere, and International Labour Office, *Workplace Violence in Service Sectors*, 15.

18. Arnette and Walsleben, "Combating Fear and Restoring Safety in Schools," quoted in Verdugo, Vere, and International Labour Office, *Workplace Violence in Service Sectors*, 15.

19. Convention on the Rights of the Child, article 19.1, 19.2, Nov. 20, 1989, 1577 United Nations Treaty Series 3.

20. Cyberbullying Research Centre, "Research."

21. Livingstone et al., *Risks and Safety on the Internet*, 6.

22. U.S. Secret Service and U.S. Department of Justice, *Final Report and Findings of the Safe School Initiative*, 21.

23. Anti–Bullying Bill of Rights Act, Assembly P.L. 2010, c.122, 3466 (United States, New Jersey 2010).

Chapter 5. The Predatory Playground of Workplaces

1.   OnRec, "Monster Global Poll," 2011.
2.   European Foundation for the Improvement of Living and Working Conditions, *Third European Working Conditions Survey*, quoted in European Foundation for the Improvement of Working and Living Conditions, *Work–Related Stress*, 2.
3.   Commission Recommendation of 19 September 2003 Concerning the European Schedule of Occupational Diseases, Annex 1, 2003 Official Journal of the European Community (L 238).
4.   International Labour Organization, *List of Occupational Diseases*.
5.   European Foundation for the Improvement of Working and Living Conditions, *Preventing Violence and Harassment*, 19.
6.   Workplace Bullying Institute, "Results of the 2010 and 2007 WBI U.S. Workplace Bullying Survey."
7.   Ibid.
8.   International Labour Organization, *Code of Practice on Workplace Violence in Services Sectors*, 4.
9.   *Report of the Expert Advisory Group on Workplace Bullying*, 11.
10. Economic and Social Research Institute et al., *Bullying in the Workplace*, 61.
11. Ibid.
12. CPTED: Mayhew, Chappell, and the ILO/ICN/WHO/PSI Joint Programme, "Workplace Violence in the Health Sector: A Case Study in Australia," 7–12.
13. Victimisation at Work Ordinance, Arbetsmiljöverket Statute Book 1993:17 (Sweden).
14. Bowie, "Defining Violence at Work," 11–20.
15. Economic and Social Research Institute et al., *Bullying in the Workplace: Survey Reports, 2007*, 42.
16. Sinclair-Bernadino, "Negligent Hiring Doctrine."
17. O'Moore, *Report on the National Survey on Workplace Bullying in Ireland*, 38.
18. McCarthy and Mayhew, *Safeguarding the Organization*, 38–58.
19. Ironside and Seifert, "Tackling Bullying in the Workplace," 390.

20. Ibid., 386.
21. Directive 89/391/EEC of 12 June 1989 on the Introduction of Measures to Encourage Improvements in the Safety and Health of Workers at Work, article 9.1. (c) 1989 Official Journal of the European Community (L 183).
22. Hoel, Sparks, and Cooper, *Cost of Violence/Stress at Work*, 5.

Chapter 6. Global Surveys on Bullying

1. Directive 89/391/EEC of 12 June 1989 on the Introduction of Measures to Encourage Improvements in the Safety and Health of Workers at Work, article 1.1, 1989 Official Journal of the European Community (L 183).
2. ACTU Occupational Health and Safety Unit and Pennicuik, *Stop Stress at Work.*
3. Chappell and Di Martino, *Violence at Work*, Third Ed., 12.
4. OnRec, "Monster Global Poll," 2011.
5. Johnston, "Workplace Bullying Trial Begins."
6. O'Moore, *Report on the National Survey on Workplace Bullying in Ireland*, 65.
7. Ministry of Health, Labour and Welfare, *Japan Individual Labour Dispute Resolution System*, 144.
8. Home Office and Upson, *Violence at Work: Findings From the 2002/2003 British Crime Survey*, 1.
9. Trades Union Congress, "E–Bulletin," *Risks* 510, 2011.
10. U.S. Department of Justice and Duhart, *Violence in the Workplace, 1993–1999*, 1.
11. National Institute for Occupational Safety and Health, *Most Workplace Bullying is Worker to Worker.*
12. Workplace Bullying Institute, "Results of the 2010 and 2007 WBI U.S. Workplace Bullying Survey."
13. Di Martino, *Workplace Violence in the Health Sector*, 16.
14. Home Office and Upson, *Violence at Work: Findings from the 2002/2003 British Crime Survey*, 9.
15. Emergency Workers (Scotland) Act, 2005, section 5 (Acts of the Scottish Parliament 2).
16. Verdugo, Vere, and International Labour Office, *Workplace Violence in Service Sectors*, 15.

Chapter 7. European Surveys Monitoring the Workplace

1.   European Foundation for the Improvement of Living and Working Conditions, *Fourth European Working Conditions Survey*, 36.
2.   European Foundation for the Improvement of Living and Working Conditions, *Fifth European Working Conditions Survey*.
3.   Ibid., Figure 2, Question on "Physical Violence."
4.   European Foundation, e-mail to publisher, June 17, 2013.
5.   Ibid., Figure 3, Question on "Bullying and Harassment."
6.   Ibid., Figure 4, Question on "Threats and Humiliating Behaviour."
7.   Ibid., Figure 5, Question on "Verbal Abuse."
8.   European Agency for Safety and Health at Work, *Annual Report 2007*, 22.

Chapter 8. Successful Career Psychopaths

1.   Cleckley, *Mask of Sanity*, 338–39.
2.   Mayhew et al., "Measuring the Extent of Impact," 117.
3.   Cleckley, *Mask of Sanity*, 338–39.
4.   Hare, "Electrodermal and Cardiovascular Correlates."
5.   European Foundation for the Improvement of Living and Working Conditions, *Third European Working Conditions Survey*, quoted in European Foundation for the Improvement of Working and Living Conditions, *Work–Related Stress*, 2.
6.   Board and Fritzon, "Disordered Personalities at Work," 20–3.
7.   Hare, *Without Conscience*, quoted in Daynes and Fellowes, *Is There a Psycho in Your Life?* 26.
8.   Raine et al., "Corpus Callosum Abnormalities," 1134–42.
9.   University of Southern California, "Study Finds Faulty Wiring in Psychopaths"; Raine et al., "Hippocampal Structural Asymmetry," 185–91.

Chapter 9. Global Legislation of Bullying

1.   King, *Wall Street Journal*, 1962.
2.   Mayhew et al., "Measuring the Extent of Impact," 130.

3. Health and Safety at Work Act, 1974, c. 37, part 1, section 2(1) (United Kingdom).

4. International Labour Organization, C111–Discrimination (Employment and Occupation) Convention, June 25, 1958, 362 United Nations Treaty Series 31.

5. International Labour Conference 101 Session, 312, ref 1848 http://www.ilo.org/ilc/ILCSessions/101stSession/reports/ reports-submitted/WCMS_174846/lang--en/index.htm.

6. Directive of the European Parliament and Council of 23 September 2002. 2002/73/EC Implementing the Principles of Equal Treatment for Men and Women regarding access to Employment, Vocational Training and Promotion, and Working Conditions. Official Journal of the European Community (L 269).

7. Ibid., amendment article 2.2.

8. Stone, "Revisiting the At–Will Employment Doctrine," 84.

9. *Work Health and Safety Act 2011* (Australia), http://www.comlaw.gov.au/Details/C2011A00137.

10. Well–Being of Workers in the Performance of their Work Act of Aug. 4, 1996 [Official Gazette of Belgium], Sep. 18, 1996 (Belgium).

11. Royal Decree Concerning the Prevention of Psychosocial Load Caused by Work, Including Violence, Harassment and Sexual Harassment at Work of May 17, 2007, [Official Gazette of Belgium], June 6, 2007 (Belgium).

12. Canada Labour Code, Revised Statutes of Canada 1985, c. L-2.

13. Workplace Psychological Harassment Prevention, Bill C-451, (Canada), http://www.parl.gc.ca/HousePublications/ Publication.aspx?Language=E&Mode=1&DocId=2333333.

14. The Occupational Health and Safety Act with Respect to Violence and Harassment in the Workplace and Other Matters, Statutes of Ontario 2009, c. 23 (Canada, Ontario), http://www.e-laws.gov.on.ca/html/source/statutes/ english/2009/elaws_src_s09023_e.htm.

15. Consolidated Danish Working Environment Act of Mar. 18, 2005, Arbejdstilsynet, no. 268 (Denmark).

16. Occupational Safety and Health Act, 2002, no. 738 (Finland), http://www.finlex.fi/en/laki/kaannokset/2002/en20020738.pdf.
17. Law 2002–73 of 17 January 2002 on Social Modernization, [J.O.] [Official Gazette of France], Jan. 18, 2002, p. 1008 (France).
18. Safety, Health and Welfare at Work Act 2005 (Act No. 10/2005) (Ireland), http://www.irishstatutebook.ie/2005/en/act/pub/0010/.
19. Working Conditions Act of Mar. 18, 1999, Staatsblad van het Koninkrijk der Nederlanden, Mar. 29, 1999, no. 184 (Netherlands).
20. Health and Safety in Employment Act 1992 of Oct. 27, 1992, no. 96 (New Zealand).
21. Harassment Act 1997 of Dec 1, 1997, no. 92 (New Zealand).
22. Working Environment Act, 2009, Arbeidslivets lover (Norway).
23. Violence and Menaces in the Working Environment Ordinance, Arbetsmiljöverket Statute Book 1993:2; Victimisation at Work Ordinance, Arbetsmiljöverket Statute Book 1993:17 (Sweden).
24. Health and Safety at Work Act, 1974, c. 37 (United Kingdom).
25. Protection from Harassment Act, 1997, c. 40 (United Kingdom).
26. Occupational Safety and Health Act 1970, 29 United States Code section 651, amended 2004 (United States).
27. Healthy Workplace Campaign, The, "Healthy Workplace Bill," http://www.healthyworkplacebill.org/.
28. Directive 89/391/EEC of 12 June 1989 on the Introduction of Measures to Encourage Improvements in the Safety and Health of Workers at Work, 1989 Official Journal of the European Community (L 183).
29. Ibid., article 6.2.(g).
30. Richard Wynne et al., *Guidance on the Prevention of Violence at Work*, quoted in Chappell and Di Martino, Violence at Work Third Ed, 280.

31. Ibid., 281.
32. Ibid.
33. Ibid.
34. Ibid.
35. European Commission Report of the Advisory Committee on Safety, Hygiene and Health Protection at Work 1564/2/01, section 2.2.7., COM (2003) 0346.
36. European Commission Communication, Adapting to Change in Work and Society: A New Community Strategy on Health and Safety at Work 2002–2006, COM (2002) 118.
37. Ibid., 12.
38. European Agency for Safety and Health at Work, *Annual Report 2007*, 22.
39. Universal Declaration of Human Rights, United Nations Doc. A/RES/217(III) (Dec. 10, 1948).
40. International Labour Organisation, Declaration of Philadelphia, 10 May, 1944, Annex 1 (a), http://www.ilo.org/dyn/normlex/en/f?p=1000:62:0::NO: 62:P62_LIST_ENTRIE_ID:2453907:NO#declaration.
41. ILO, Protocol to the Occupational Safety and Health Convention, 1981, article 1.(b), 2308 United Nations Treaty Series.
42. World Health Organization, *World Report on Violence and Health*, 5.

Chapter 10. Making a Claim

No references.

Chapter 11. Bullying of the Elderly

1. World Health Organization, *World Report on Violence and Health*, 126–7.
2. Ibid., 130.
3. Pillemer and Finkelhor,"Prevalence of Elder Abuse," 51–7.
4. Podnieks, "National Survey on Abuse of the Elderly in Canada," 5–58.
5. Kivelä et al., "Abuse in Old Age," 1–18.
6. Ogg and Bennett, "Elder Abuse in Britain," 998–9.
7. Comijs et al., "Elder Abuse in the Community," 885–8.

8. United Nations, World "Elder Abuse Awareness Day," 15 June.

9. European Standards, "Services Offered by Hearing Aid Professionals."

10. Pillemer and Finkelhor,"Prevalence of Elder Abuse," 51–7.

11. Pillemer and Moore, "Highlights From a Study of Abuse," quoted in World Health Organization, *World Report on Violence and Health*, 130.

12. Universal Declaration of Human Rights, article 1, United Nations Doc. A/RES/217(III) (Dec. 10, 1948).

13. Implementation of the International Plan of Action on Ageing and Related Activities, United Nations Doc. A/RES/46/91 (Dec. 16, 1991).

14. World Health Organization, *World Report on Violence and Health*, 141–3.

15. United Nations, *World Population Prospects: The 2006 Revision*, 6–9.

16. Eurostat and Giannakouris, *Ageing Characterises the Demographic Perspectives of the European Societies*, 1.

Chapter 12. Institutional Bullying

1. Ryan, *Bullies, Victims and Bystanders*, 95.

2. United Nations ESCAP, "What is Good Governance?"

3. Transparency International, *Corruption Perception Index*.

4. O'Connell, Pepler, and Craig, "Peer Involvement in Bullying," 438.

5. Infoplease, "World's Ten Most Corrupt Leaders."

6. *Merriam-Webster OnLine*, s.v. "Kleptocracy," http://www.merriam-webster.com/dictionary/ kleptocracy.

7. Hobbes, *Leviathan*, 56–7.

8. Liefooghe and Mackenzie Davey, "Accounts of Workplace Bullying," 375–92.

9. United Nations, "Anti–Corruption Day," 9 December.

10. United Nations Convention Against Corruption, Oct. 31, 2003, 2349 United Nations Treaty Series 41.

11. *Merriam-Webster OnLine*, s.v. "Underdog," http://www.merriam-webster.com/dictionary/underdog.

12. McCarthy and Mayhew, *Safeguarding the Organization*, 214–5.
13. Macdonald, "NHS Whistleblowers."

Chapter 13. The Price of Psychosocial Behaviour
1. Hoel, Sparks, and Cooper, *Cost of Violence/Stress at Work*, 5.
2. Neuberger, *Mobbing: Übel mitspielen in Organisationen*, 95, quoted in Lorho and Hilp, "Bullying at Work," 14.
3. Levi and Lunde-Jensen, *"A Model for Assessing the Costs of Stressors"* quoted in Hoel, Sparks, and Cooper, *Cost of Violence/Stress at Work*, 25.
4. Einarsen et al., "Concept of Bullying at Work," quoted in Chappell and Di Martino, *Violence at Work*, Third Ed., 141.
5. Philbrick et al., "Workplace Violence: The Legal Costs," 84.
6. McCarthy and Mayhew, *Safeguarding the Organization*, 43.
7. European Foundation for the Improvement of Living and Working Conditions, *Second European Survey on Working Conditions in the European Union*, quoted in Lorho and Hilp, "Bullying at Work," 12.
8. Kivimäki, Elovainio, and Vahtera, "Workplace Bullying and Sickness Absence in Hospital Staff," 658.
9. Directive 89/391/EEC of 12 June 1989 on the Introduction of Measures to Encourage Improvements in the Safety and Health of Workers at Work, 1989 article 9.1.(c), 1989 Official Journal of the European Community (L 183).
10. Health and Safety Authority, "Bullying in the Workplace: Is it a Problem?" quoted in Lorho and Hilp, "Bullying at Work," 14.
11. UNISON, *Members' Experience of Bullying at Work*, quoted in Hoel, Sparks, and Cooper, *Cost of Violence/Stress at Work,* 32.
12. Hoel, Sparks, and Cooper, *Cost of Violence/Stress at Work*, 48.
13. Hoel and Cooper, *Destructive Conflict*, quoted in Hoel, Sparks, and Cooper, *Cost of Violence/Stress at Work*, 48.
14. Hoel and Cooper, "Working with Victims," quoted in Hoel, Sparks, and Cooper, *Cost of Violence/Stress at Work*, 33.
15. Earnshaw and Cooper, *Stress and Employer Liability*, quoted in Hoel, Sparks, and Cooper, *Cost of Violence/Stress at Work*, 30.

16. Standing and Nicolini, *Review of Workplace Related Violence*, quoted in Hoel, Sparks, and Cooper, *Cost of Violence/Stress at Work*, 34.
17. Cartwright and Cooper, *Managing Workplace Stress*, 39.
18. Mayhew et al., "Measuring the Extent of Impact," 130.
19. Verdugo, Vere, and International Labour Office, *Workplace Violence in Service Sectors*, 17.
20. Neuberger, *Mobbing: Übel mitspielen in Organisationen*, 95, quoted in Lorho and Hilp, "Bullying at Work," 14.
21. Chappell and Di Martino, *Violence at Work*, Third Ed., 123.
22. U.S. Secret Service, "Preventing School Shootings," 14.
23. International Monetary Fund, "Globalization: Threat or Opportunity?" Section IV.
24. OECD Head Office, e-mail to author, October 31, 2012.

Chapter 14. The Role of Trade Unions

1. International Trade Union Confederation, "Annual Survey of Violation of Trade Union Rights 2012."
2. International Trade Union Confederation, "About Us."
3. European Foundation for the Improvement of Living and Working Conditions and Carley, *Trade Union Membership 2003–2008*, 23.
4. Ibid., 9.

Chapter 15. Cultural Changes and Power Shift

1. International Labour Conference 101 Session, 312, ref 1848 http://www.ilo.org/ilc/ILCSessions/101stSession/reports/reports-submitted/WCMS_174846/lang--en/index.htm.
2. Hoel, Sparks, and Cooper, *Cost of Violence/Stress at Work*, 5.
3. International Labour Organization, *List of Occupational Diseases*.
4. European Agency for Safety and Health at Work, *Annual Report 2007*, 22.
5. Commission Recommendation of 19 September 2003 Concerning the European Schedule of Occupational Diseases, Annex 1, 2003 Official Journal of the European Community (L 238).
6. United Nations ESCAP, "What is Good Governance?"

BIBLIOGRAPHY ⟳

ACTU. Australian Council of Trade Unions.Occupational Health and Safety Unit. http://www.actu.org.au/

Arnette, June L., and Marjorie C. Walsleben. "Combating Fear and Restoring Safety in Schools." *Juvenile Justice Bulletin* (1998). Quoted in Richard Verdugo, Anamaria Vere, and International Labour Office. *Workplace Violence in Service Sectors with Implications for the Education Sector: Issues, Solutions and Resources.* Working Paper no. 208. Geneva: ILO, 2003.

Aronson, Elliot. *Nobody Left to Hate: Teaching Compassion After Columbine.* New York: W.H. Freeman, 2000.

Badura, Bernhard, Henner Schellschmidt, and Christian Vetter. *Fehlzeiten–Report 2003 Wettbewerbsfaktor Work–Life–Balance.* Berlin: Springer Verlag, 2004. Quoted in European Foundation for the Improvement of Living and Working Conditions. *Work–Related Stress.* Dublin: Eurofound, 2007. http://www.eurofound.europa.eu/ewco/reports/TN0502TR01/TN0502TR01.htm.

Board, Belinda J., and Katarina Fritzon."Disordered Personalities at Work." *Psychology, Crime and Law* 11, no. 1 (2005): 17–32.

Bowie, Vaughan. "Defining Violence at Work: A New Typology." In *Violence at Work: Causes, Patterns and Prevention*, edited by Martin Gill, Bonnie S. Fisher and Vaughan Bowie, 1–20. Cullompton: Willan, 2002.

BSI. "Guidance on the Management of Psychosocial Risks in the Workplace." PAS 1010: 2011.

Canadian Centre for Justice Statistics. "Youth Violent Crime." *Juristat* 19, no. 13 (1999). Quoted in Richard Verdugo, Anamaria Vere, and International Labour Office.

Workplace Violence in Service Sectors with Implications for the Education Sector: Issues, Solutions and Resources. Working Paper no. 208. Geneva: International Labour Office, 2003.

Cartwright, Susan, and Cary L. Cooper. *Managing Workplace Stress.* California: Sage Publications, 1997.

Chappell, Duncan, and Vittorio Di Martino. *Violence at Work.* Third Ed. Geneva: International Labour Office, 2006.

Child Health Promotion Research Center (CHPRC). http://www.chprc.ecu.edu.au/resources/.

Cleckley, Hervey. *The Mask of Sanity: An Attempt to Clarify Some Issues About the So Called Psychopathic Personality.* 5th ed. William A Dolan, 1988.

Comijs, Hannie C., Anne M. Pot, Johannes H. Smit, Lex M. Bouter, and Cees Jonker. "Elder Abuse in the Community: Prevalence and Consequences." *Journal of the American Geriatrics Society* 46, no. 7 (1998): 885–8.

Commission Recommendation of 19 September 2003 Concerning the European Schedule of Occupational Diseases, Annex 1, 2003 Official Journal of the European Community (L 238). http://eurlex.europa.eu/LexUriServ/LexUriServ.do?uri=CELEX:32003H0670:EN:HTML.

Cowie, Helen, Paul Naylor, Ian Rivers, Peter K. Smith, and Beatriz Pereira. "Measuring Workplace Bullying." *Aggression and Violent Behavior* 7, no. 1 (2002): 33–51.

CSA. "Psychological Health and Safety in the Workplace Prevention, Promotion, and Guidance to Staged Implementation." CAN/CSA–Z1003–13/BNQ 9700–803/2013.

http://shop.csa.ca/en/canada/occupational-health-and-safety-management/cancsa-z1003-13bnq-9700-8032013/invt/z10032013.

Cyberbullying Research Center. "Research." http://www.cyberbullying.us/research/.

Darley, John M., and Bibb Latané. "Bystander Intervention in Emergencies: Diffusion of Responsibility." *Journal of Personality and Social Psychology* 8, no. 4 (1968): 377–83.

Di Martino, Vittorio. *Workplace Violence in the Health Sector: Country Case Studies: Brazil, Bulgaria, Lebanon, Portugal, South Africa, Thailand and an Additional Australian Study: Synthesis Report.* The ILO, ICN, PSI, WHO Joint Programme, 2002. http://www.who.int/violence_injury_prevention/injury/en/WVsynthesisreport.pdf.

Due, Pernille, Bjørn E. Holstein, John Lynch, Finn Diderichsen, Saoirse Nic Gabhain, Peter Scheidt, Candace Currie, and the Health Behaviour in School–Aged Children Bullying Working Group. "Bullying and Symptoms Among School–Aged Children: International Comparative Cross Sectional Study in 28 Countries." *European Journal of Public Health* 15, no. 2 (2005): 128–32.

Earnshaw, Jill, and Cary L. Cooper. *Stress and Employer Liability.* London: Chartered Institute of Personnel and Development, 1996. Quoted in Helge Hoel, Kate Sparks, and Cary L. Cooper. *The Cost of Violence/Stress at Work and the Benefits of a Violence/Stress–Free Working Environment.* Manchester: UMIST; Geneva: International Labour Organization, 2001.

Economic and Social Research Institute, Philip O'Connell, Emma Calvert, and Dorothy Watson. *Bullying in the Workplace: Survey Reports, 2007.* Dublin: Department of Enterprise, Trade and Employment, 2007

http://www.djei.ie/publications/employment/2007/
esrireportbullying.pdf.

Einarsen, Ståle, Helge Hoel, Dieter Zapf, and Cary L. Cooper. "The Concept of Bullying at Work: The European Tradition." In *Bullying and Emotional Abuse in the Workplace*, edited by Ståle Einarsen, Helge Hoel, Dieter Zapf, and Cary L. Cooper, 3–30. London: Taylor and Francis, 2003. Quoted in Duncan Chappell and Vittorio Di Martino. *Violence at Work*. Third Ed. Geneva: International Labour Office, 2006.

Einarsen, Ståle, and Eva G. Mikkelsen. "Individual Effects of Exposure to Bullying at Work." In *Bullying and Emotional Abuse in the Workplace*, edited by Ståle Einarsen, Helge Hoel, Dieter Zapf, and Cary L. Cooper, 127–44. London: Taylor and Francis, 2003.

Einarsen, Ståle, Bjørn Inge Raknes, and Stig Matthiesen. "Mobbing og personkonflikter: Helsefarlig samspill på arbeidsplassen" [Bullying and Personified Conflicts: Health–Endangering Interaction at Work]. Bergen, Norway: Sigma Forlag, 1994. Quoted in Charlotte Rayner, Helge Hoel, and Cary L. Cooper. *Workplace Bullying: What We Know, Who is to Blame, and What Can We Do?* London: Taylor and Francis, 2001.

Einarsen, Ståle, Bjørn Inge Raknes, and Stig Matthiesen. "Mobbing og personkonflikter: Helsefarlig samspill på arbeidsplassen" [Bullying and Personified Conflicts: Health Endangering Interaction at Work]. Quoted in Ståle Einarsen and Eva G. Mikkelsen. "Individual Effects of Exposure to Bullying at Work." In *Bullying and Emotional Abuse in the Workplace*, edited by Ståle Einarsen, Helge Hoel, Dieter Zapf, and Cary L. Cooper, 127–44. London: Taylor and Francis, 2003.

European Agency for Safety and Health at Work,

Work–Related Stress. Cox, Tom, Amanda Griffiths, and Eusebio Rial-González. *Research on Work–Related Stress.* Luxembourg: Office for Official Publications of the European Communities, 2000. http://osha.europa.eu/en/publications/reports/ 203/.

—. 2007 *Annual Report 2007.* Luxembourg: Office for Official Publications of the European Communities, 2008. ISSN 1681–0155. https://osha.europa.eu/en/publications/corporate/ 2007full/.

European Foundation for the Improvement of Living and Working Conditions. Dublin, 1996. Pascal Paoli. *Second European Survey on Working Conditions in the European Union.* http://www.eurofound.europa.eu/pubdocs/1997/26/en/ 1/ef9726en.pdf.

—. 1996. Pascal Paoli. *Second European Survey on Working Conditions in the European Union.* http://www.eurofound.europa.eu/pubdocs/1997/26/en/ 1/ef9726en.pdf. Quoted in Frank Lorho and Ulrich Hilp. "Bullying at Work." Working Paper SOCI 108 EN. European Parliament, 2001. http://edz.bib.uni-mannheim.de/www-edz/pdf/dg4/ SOCI108_EN.pdf.

—. 2000. *Third European Working Conditions Survey 2000.* Pascal Paoli and Damien Merllié. http://www.eurofound.europa.eu/publications/htmlfiles /ef0121.htm.

—. 2003. *Preventing Violence and Harassment in the Workplace* Di Martino, Vittorio, Helge Hoel, Cary L. Cooper. www.eurofound.europa.eu/pubdocs/2002/109/en/1/ ef02109en.pdf.

—.   2005. *Fourth European Working Conditions Survey 2005.*
        Agnès Parent-Thirion, Enrique Macías Fernández, John
        Hurley, and Greet Vermeylen.
        http://www.eurofound.europa.eu/pubdocs/2006/98/
        en/2/ef0698en.pdf.

—.   2007. *Work–Related Stress.*
        http://www.eurofound.europa.eu/ewco/reports/
        TN0502TR01/TN0502TR01.pdf.

—.   2009. *Trade Union Membership 2003–2008.* Mark Carley.
        Warwick: Spire Associates/IRRU, University of Warwick.
        http://www.eurofound.europa.eu/eiro/studies/
        tn0904019s/ tn0904019s.htm.

—.   2010. *Fifth European Working Conditions Survey 2010.*
        Agnès Parent-Thirion, Greet Vermeylen, Gijs van
        Houten, Maija Lyly-Yrjänäinen, Isabella Biletta, and Jorge
        Cabrita.   http://www.eurofound.europa.eu/pubdocs/
        2011/82/en/1/EF1182EN.pdf.

—.   2010. European Working Conditions Survey Results.
        "(Q70a) Have You Been Subjected to Verbal Abuse at
        Work in the Last Month?" Bar chart. November 15,
        2010.   http://www.eurofound.europa.eu/surveys/smt/
        ewcs/ewcs2010_13_03.htm.

        "(Q70c) Have You Been Subjected to Threats and
        Humiliating Behaviour at Work in the Last Month?" Bar
        chart. November 15, 2010.
        http://www.eurofound.europa.eu/surveys/smt/ewcs/ew
        cs2010_13_04.htm.

        "(Q71a) Have You Been Subjected to Physical Violence
        at Work in the Past Year?" Bar chart. November 15,
        2010.   http://www.eurofound.europa.eu/surveys/smt/
        ewcs/ewcs2010_13_05.htm.

"(Q71b) Have You Been Subjected to Bullying and Harassment at Work in the Past Year?" Bar chart. November 15, 2010.
http://www.eurofound.europa.eu/surveys/smt/ewcs/ewcs2010_13_06.htm.

European Standards. "Services Offered by Hearing Aid Professionals." CSN EN 15927: 2010.

Eurostat and Konstantinos Giannakouris. *Ageing Characterises the Demographic Perspectives of the European Societies.* Eurostat: Statistics in Focus, 2008.
http://epp.eurostat.ec.europa.eu/cache/ITY_OFFPUB/KS-SF-08-072/EN /KS-SF-08-072-EN.PDF.

Farrington, David P. "Understanding and Preventing Bullying." *Crime and Justice* 17 (1993): 381–458.

Golding, William. *Lord of the Flies.* London: Faber and Faber, 1954.

Hare, Robert D. "Electrodermal and Cardiovascular Correlates of Psychopathy." In *Psychopathic Behaviour Approaches to Research,* edited by Robert D. Hare and Daisy Schalling, 107–44. Chicester, England: John Wiley and Sons, 1978.

Hare, Robert D. *Without Conscience: The Disturbing World of the Psychopaths Among Us.* New York: The Guilford Press, 1999. Quoted in Kerry Daynes and Jessica Fellowes. *Is There a Psycho in Your Life?* London: Coronet, 2012.

Hawton, Keith. "Assessment of Suicide Risk." *The British Journal of Psychiatry* 150 (1987): 145–53. Quoted in Charlotte Rayner, Helge Hoel, and Cary L. Cooper. *Workplace Bullying: What We Know, Who is to Blame, and What Can We Do?* London: Taylor and Francis, 2001.

Health and Safety Authority. "Bullying in the Workplace: Is it a Problem?" *Health and Safety Authority Newsletter* January/ February (1998). Quoted in Frank Lorho and Ulrich Hilp. "Bullying at Work." Working Paper SOCI 108 EN. European Parliament, 2001. http://edz.bib.uni-mannheim.de/www-edz/pdf/dg4/ SOCI108_EN.pdf.

Healthy Workplace Campaign, The. "The Healthy Workplace Bill." http://www.healthyworkplacebill.org/.

Hobbes, Thomas. *Leviathan.* Third Ed. Digireads.com Publishing, 2009.

Hoel, Helge, and Cary L. Cooper. *Destructive Conflict and Bullying at Work.* Unpublished Report. Manchester: UMIST, 2000. Quoted in Helge Hoel, Kate Sparks, and Cary L. Cooper. *The Cost of Violence/Stress at Work and the Benefits of a Violence/Stress–Free Working Environment.* Geneva: International Labour Organization, 2001.

Hoel, Helge, and Cary L. Cooper. "Working with Victims of Workplace Bullying." In *Good Practice in Working with Victims of Violence,* edited by Hazel Kemshall and Jacki Pritchard, 101-18. London: Jessica Kingsley Publishers, 2000. Quoted in Helge Hoel, Kate Sparks, and Cary L. Cooper. *The Cost of Violence/Stress at Work and the Benefits of a Violence/Stress–Free Working Environment.* Geneva: International Labour Organization, 2001.

Hoel, Helge, Kate Sparks, and Cary L. Cooper. *The Cost of Violence/Stress at Work and the Benefits of a Violence/Stress– Free Working Environment.* Geneva: International Labour Organization, 2001.

Home Office and Anna Upson. *Violence at Work: Findings From the 2002/2003 British Crime Survey.* Report 04/04. Home

Office, 2004. http://workboostwales.net/violence/bcsviolence0203.pdf.

Infoplease. "World's Ten Most Corrupt Leaders." Pearson Education, 2007. http://www.infoplease.com/ipa/A0921295.html.

International Trade Union Confederation,"Annual Survey of Violation of Trade Union Rights 2012." http://survey.ituc-csi.org/.

International Labour Organization. *Code of Practice on Workplace Violence in Services Sectors and Measures to Combat this Phenomenon.* Geneva: International Labour Office, 2003. http://www.ilo.org/wcmsp5/groups/public/---ed_protect/---protrav/---safework/documents/normativeinstrument/wcms_107705.pdf.

—. 2010. *List of Occupational Diseases, Revised 2010.* Occupational Safety and Health Series, no. 74. Geneva: International Labour Office, 2010. http//www.ilo.org/global/publications/books/WCMS_150323/lang--en/index.htm.

International Monetary Fund. "Globalization: Threat or Opportunity?" April 12, 2000. http://www.imf.org/external/np/exr/ib/2000/041200to.htm.

International Trade Union Confederation. "About Us." http://www.ituc-csi.org/ about-us.

Ironside, Mike, and Roger Seifert. "Tackling Bullying in the Workplace: The Collective Dimension." In *Bullying and Emotional Abuse in the Workplace*, edited by Ståle Einarsen,

Helge Hoel, Dieter Zapf, and Cary L. Cooper, 383–98. London: Taylor and Francis, 2003.

Johnson, David W., and Roger T. Johnson. "Why Violence Prevention Programs Don't Work–and What Does." *Educational Leadership* 52, no. 5 (1995): 63–8.

Johnston, Vanessa. "Workplace Bullying Trial Begins." *Deutsche Welle*. January 20, 2010. http://www.dw.de/workplace-bullying-trial-begins/a-5150735–1.

King, Martin Luther. *Wall Street Journal.* November 13, 1962.

Kivelä, Sirkka-Liisa, Päivi Köngäs-Saviaro, Erkki Kesti, Kimmo Pahkala, and Maija-Liisa Ijäs. "Abuse in Old Age: Epidemiological Data from Finland." *Journal of Elder Abuse and Neglect* 4, no. 3 (1992): 1–18.

Kivimäki, Mika, Marko Elovainio, and Jussi Vahtera. "Workplace Bullying and Sickness Absence in Hospital Staff." *Occupational and Environment Medicine* 57, no. 10 (2000): 656–60.

Koningsveld, Ernst, Wim Zwinkels, Jos Mossink, X.M Thie and Marien Abspoel. *Societal Costs of Working Conditions of Employees in 2001*. The Hague: Ministry of Social Affairs and Employment, 2001. Quoted in European Foundation for the Improvement of Living and Working Conditions. *Work–Related Stress*. Dublin: Eurofound, 2007. http://www.eurofound.europa.eu/ewco/reports/TN0502TR01/TN0502TR01.htm.

Leymann, Heinz. "Mobbing and Psychological Terror at Workplaces." *Violence and Victims* 5, no. 2 (1990): 119–26. Quoted in Duncan Chappell and Vittorio Di Martino. *Violence at Work*. Third Ed. Geneva: International Labour Office, 2006.

Leymann, Heinz, and Annelie Gustafsson. "Mobbing at Work and the Development of Post–Traumatic Stress Disorders." *European Journal of Work and Organizational Psychology* 5, no. 2 (1996): 251–76. Quoted in European Foundation for the Improvement of Living and Working Conditions. *Preventing Violence and Harassment in the Workplace.* Dublin: European Foundation for the Improvement of Living and Working Conditions, 2003. www.eurofound.europa.eu/pubdocs/2002/109/en/1/ ef02109en.pdf.

Liefooghe, Andreas, and Kate Mackenzie Davey. "Accounts of Workplace Bullying: The Role of the Organization." *European Journal of Work and Organizational Psychology* 10, no. 4 (2001): 375–92.

Levi, Lenart. & Lunde-Jensen, Per. (1995) *A Model for Assessing the Costs of Stressors at National Level: Socio-Economic Costs of Stress in Two EU Member States.* Dublin: European Foundation for the Improvement of Living and Working Conditions.

Livingstone, Sonia, Leslie Haddon, Anke Görzig, Kjartan Ólafsson, and EU Kids Online Network. *Risks and Safety on the Internet: The Perspective of European Children Initial Findings From the EU Kids Online Survey of 9–16 Year Olds and their Parents.* London: EU Kids Online, 2010. http://www2.cnrs.fr/sites/en/fichier/rapport_english.pdf.

Lorho, Frank, and Ulrich Hilp. "Bullying at Work." Working Paper SOCI 108 EN. European Parliament, 2001. http://edz.bib.uni-mannheim.de/www-edz/pdf/dg4/ SOCI108_EN.pdf.

Lösel, Friedrich, and Thomas Bliesener. "Germany." In *The Nature of School Bullying: A Cross–National Perspective*, edited by Peter K. Smith, Yohji Morita, Josine Junger-Tas, Dan Olweus, Richard F. Catalano, and Philip Slee, 224–49.

New York: Routledge, 1999. Quoted in Richard Verdugo, Anamaria Vere, and International Labour Office. *Workplace Violence in Service Sectors with Implications for the Education Sector: Issues, Solutions and Resources.* Working Paper no. 208. Geneva: International Labour Office, 2003.

Macdonald, Victoria. "NHS Whistleblowers: Are They Really Being Protected Now?" *Channel 4 News.* May 13, 2013. http://www.channel4.com/news/nhs-whistleblowers-are-they-really-being-protected-now.

Mayhew, Claire, Duncan Chappell, and the ILO/ICN/ WHO/ /PSI Joint Programme on Workplace Violence in the Health Sector. "Workplace Violence in the Health Sector: A Case Study in Australia." *Journal of Occupational Health and Safety – Australia And New Zealand* 19, no. 6 (2003): 1–40.

Mayhew, Claire, Paul McCarthy, Duncan Chappell, Michael Quinlan, Michelle Barker, and Michael Sheehan. "Measuring the Extent of Impact from Occupational Violence and Bullying on Traumatised Workers." *Employee Responsibilities and Rights Journal* 16, no. 3 (2004): 117–34.

McCarthy, Paul, and Claire Mayhew. *Safeguarding the Organization Against Violence and Bullying: An International Perspective.* Houndmills, Basingstoke, Hampshire: Palgrave Macmillan, 2004.

Mikkelsen Eva and Einarsen, Ståle, "Basic Assumptions and symptoms of post traumatic stress among victims of bullying at work," *European Journal of Work and Organisational Psychology.* Vol.11, 2002, 87–111.

Ministry of Health, Labour and Welfare. Japan. *Individual Labour Dispute Resolution System.* 143–44. http://www.mhlw.go.jp/

english/wp/wp-hw5/dl/23010410e.pdf.

National Institute for Occupational Safety and Health. *Most Workplace Bullying is Worker to Worker, Early Findings from NIOSH Study Suggest.* (202) 401–3749. July 28, 2004. http://www.cdc.gov/niosh/updates/upd-07-28-04.html.

Neuberger, Oswald. *Mobbing: Übel mitspielen in Organisationen.* Munich: Hampp, 1999. Quoted in Frank Lorho and Ulrich Hilp. "Bullying at Work." Working Paper SOCI 108 EN. European Parliament, 2001. http://edz.bib.uni-mannheim.de/www-edz/pdf/dg4/SOCI108_EN.pdf.

O'Connell, Paul, Debra Pepler, and Wendy Craig. "Peer Involvement in Bullying: Insights and Challenges for Intervention." *Journal of Adolescence* 22, no. 4 (1999): 437–52.

Ogg, Jim, and Gary Bennett. "Elder Abuse in Britain." *British Medical Journal* 305, no. 6860 (1992): 998–9.

Olweus, Dan. "Bully/Victim Problems Among School Children: Basic Facts and Effects of a School–Based Intervention Program." In *The Development and Treatment of Childhood Aggression,* edited by Debra Pepler and Kenneth Rubin, 411–48. Hillsdale, NJ: Lawrence Erlbaum Associates, 1991. Quoted in Margaret Hodgins. "Taking a Health Promotion Approach to the Problem of Bullying." *International Journal of Psychology and Psychological Therapy* 8, no. 1 (2008): 13–23.

Olweus, Dan. "Recognizing Bullying." Violence Prevention Works! Hazelden, 2013. http://www.violencepreventionworks.org/public/recognizing_bullying.page.

O' Moore, Mona. *Report on the National Survey on Workplace Bullying in Ireland*. Dublin: Trinity College Dublin, 2000.

OnRec. "Monster Global Poll Reveals Workplace Bullying is Endemic." *The Online Recruitment Resource*. June 10, 2011. http://www.onrec.com/news/news-archive/monster-global-poll-reveals-workplace-bullying-is-endemic.

Ortega, Rosario, and Joaquin A. Mora-Merchan. "Spain." In *The Nature of School Bullying: A Cross–National Perspective*, edited by Peter K. Smith, Yohji Morita, Josine Junger-Tas, Dan Olweus, Richard F. Catalano, and Philip Slee, 157–73. New York: Routledge, 1999. Quoted in Richard Verdugo, Anamaria Vere, and International Labour Office. *Workplace Violence in Service Sectors with Implications for the Education Sector: Issues, Solutions and Resources*. Working Paper no. 208. Geneva: International Labour Office, 2003.

Pepler, Debra J., and Wendy Craig. *Making a Difference in Bullying*. (No. 60). Toronto, Canada: York University, LaMarsh Centre for Research on Violence and Conflict Resolution, 2000.

Philbrick, Jane, Marcia Sparks, Marsha Hass, and Steven Arsenault. "Workplace Violence: The Legal Costs Can Kill You." *American Business Review* 21, no. 1 (2003): 84–90.

Pillemer, Karl, and David Finkelhor. "The Prevalence of Elder Abuse: A Random Sample Survey." *Gerontologist* 28, no. 1 (1988): 51–7.

Pillemer, Karl, and David W. Moore. "Highlights From a Study of Abuse of Patients in Nursing Homes." *Journal of Elder Abuse and Neglect* 2, no. 1–2 (1990): 5–30.

Podnieks, Elizabeth. "National Survey on Abuse of the Elderly in Canada." *Journal of Elder Abuse and Neglect* 4, no. 1–2 (1992): 5–58.

Poland, Blake D., Lawrence W. Green, and Irving Rootman. *Settings for Health Promotion: Linking Theory and Practice.* California: Sage Publications, 2000.

Quine, Lyn. "Workplace Bullying in NHS Community Trust: Staff Questionnaire Survey." *BMJ* 318, no. 7178 (1999): 228–32. Quoted in Charlotte Rayner, Helge Hoel, and Cary L. Cooper. *Workplace Bullying: What We Know, Who is to Blame, and What Can We Do?* London: Taylor and Francis, 2001.

Raine, Adrian, Sharon Ishikawa, Estibaliz Arce, Todd Lencz, Kevin H. Knuth, Susan Bihrle, Lori Lacasse, and Patrick Colletti. "Hippocampal Structural Asymmetry in Unsuccessful Psychopaths." *Biological Psychiatry* 55, no. 2 (2004): 185–91.

Raine, Adrian, Todd Lencz, Kristen Taylor, Joseph B. Hellige, Susan Bihrle, Lori Lacasse, Mimi Lee, Sharon Ishikawa, and Patrick Colletti. "Corpus Callosum Abnormalities in Psychopathic Antisocial Individuals." *Archives of General Psychiatry* 60, no. 11 (2003): 1134–42.

Report of the Expert Advisory Group on Workplace Bullying. Dublin: The Stationary Office, 2001. http://www.djei.ie/ publications/employment/2005/bullying.pdf.

Rigby, Ken. "The Relationship Between Reported Health and Involvement in Bully/ Victim Problems Among Male and Female Secondary Schoolchildren." *Journal of Health Psychology* 3, no. 4 (1998): 465–76. doi:10.1177/1359105 39800300402.

Rigby, Ken, and Philip Slee. "Australia." In *The Nature of School*

Bullying: A Cross-National Perspective, edited by Peter K. Smith, Yohji Morita, Josine Junger-Tas, Dan Olweus, Richard F. Catalano, and Philip Slee, 324–39. New York: Routledge, 1999. Quoted in Richard Verdugo, Anamaria Vere, and International Labour Office. *Workplace Violence in Service Sectors with Implications for the Education Sector: Issues, Solutions and Resources*. Working Paper no. 208. Geneva: International Labour Office, 2003.

Roosevelt, Eleanor. [Free Standing Quotation]. *The Reader's Digest* 37 (September 1940): 84.

Ryan, Terri. *Bullies, Victims and Bystanders*. International Development and Information Guides, 2011.

Saskatchewan Teachers' Association. "Survey Finds Teacher Abuse Growing." *Saskatchewan Bulletin*, May 13, 1994.

Sebastián García, Olga. "Los riesgos psicosociales y su prevención: mobbing, estrés y otros problemas" [Psychosocial Risks and Their Prevention: Mobbing, Stress and Other Problems]. Paper presented at the Technical Seminar on Prevention of Psychosocial Risks, Spanish National Institute of Safety and Hygiene at Work. Madrid, October 2002. Quoted in European Foundation for the Improvement of Living and Working Conditions. *Work-Related Stress*. Dublin: Eurofound, 2007. http://www.eurofound.europa.eu/ewco/reports/TN0502TR01/TN0502TR01.htm.

Sharp, Sonia, and Peter K. Smith. *Tackling Bullying in Your School: A Practical Handbook for Teachers*. London: Routledge, 1991. Quoted in Richard Verdugo, Anamaria Vere, and International Labour Office. *Workplace Violence in Service Sectors with Implications for the Education Sector: Issues, Solutions and Resources*. Working Paper no. 208. Geneva: International Labour Office, 2003.

Sinclair-Bernadino, Linnea. "Negligent Hiring Doctrine Opens More Doors for Pre-Employment Screening." Island Investigations. 2006. http://www.pimall.com/nais/n.hire.html.

Standing, Hilary, and Davide Nicolini. *Review of Workplace Related Violence.* London: Health and Safety Executive/HSMO, 1997. Quoted in Helge Hoel, Kate Sparks, and Cary L. Cooper. *The Cost of Violence/Stress at Work and the Benefits of a Violence/Stress–Free Working Environment.* Geneva: International Labour Organization, 2001.

Stone, Katherine V.W. "Revisiting the At–Will Employment Doctrine: Imposed Terms, Implied Terms, and the Normative World of the Workplace." *Industrial Law Journal* 36, no. 1 (2007): 84–101.

Trades Union Congress. "E–Bulletin." *Risks* 510. June 18 2011. http://www.tuc.org.uk/workplace/tuc-19681-f0.cfm.

Transparency International. *Corruption Perception Index.* 2012. http://www.transparency.org/research/cpi/overview.

Thylefors, Ingela. *Syndabockar: Om utstötning och mobbning i arbetslivet.* Stockholm, Sweden: Naturoch Kultur, 1987. Quoted in Einarsen, Stale, and Eva G. Mikkelsen. Quoted in *"Individual Effects of Exposure to Bullying at Work."*

UNISON. *Members' Experience of Bullying at Work.* London: UNISON, 1997. Quoted in Helge Hoel, Kate Sparks, and Cary L. Cooper. *The Cost of Violence/Stress at Work and the Benefits of a Violence/Stress–Free Working Environment.* Geneva: International Labour Organization, 2001.

United Nations. "Anti–Corruption Day." 9 December. http://www.un.org/en/events/anticorruptionday/.

—.   "Elder Abuse Awareness Day." 15 June.
        http://www.un.org/en/events/elderabuse/.

—.   ESCAP. "What is Good Governance?"
        http://www.unescap.org/huset/gg/governance.html.

—.   2003 "United Nations Convention Against Corruption,"
        (Vienna: UN Office on Drugs and Crime, 2004),
        http://www.unodc.org/documents/treaties/UNCAC/
        Publications/Convention/08-50026_E.pdf.

—.   2006. *World Population Prospects: The 2006 Revision.* New
        York: United Nations, 2007.
        http://www.un.org/esa/population/publications/
        wpp2006/WPP2006_Highlights_rev.pdf.

U.S. Department of Education, U.S. Department of Justice,
        Rachel Dinkes, Jana Kemp, and Katrina Baum. *Indicators
        of School Crime and Safety: 2009.* (NCES 2010–012/NCJ
        228478). Washington, D.C.: U.S. Department of
        Education, and Bureau of Justice Statistics Office of
        Justice Programs, 2009.

U.S. Department of Justice, Bureau of Justice Assistance, and
        Margaret Shaw. *Promoting Safety in Schools: International
        Experience and Action.* Washington, D.C.: U.S. Department
        of Justice, 2001. Quoted in Richard Verdugo, Anamaria
        Vere, and International Labour Office. *Workplace Violence
        in Service Sectors with Implications for the Education Sector:
        Issues, Solutions and Resources.* Working Paper no. 208.
        Geneva: International Labour Office, 2003.

U.S. Department of Justice and Detis Duhart. *Violence in the
        Workplace, 1993–1999.* (NCJ 190076). Bureau of Justice
        http://bjs.ojp.usdoj.gov/content/pub/pdf/vw99.pdf

U.S. Department of Justice Office of Community Oriented

Policing Services and Rana Sampson. "Bullying in Schools." *Problem Oriented Guides for Police Series* 12 (2002). http://www.cops.usdoj.gov/pdf/e12011405.pdf.

U.S. Secret Service. "Preventing School Shootings: A Summary of a U.S. Secret Service Safe School Initiative Report." *National Institute of Justice Journal* 248 (2002): 10–5. https://www.ncjrs.gov/pdffiles1/jr000248c.pdf.

U.S. Secret Service and U.S. Department of Justice. *The Final Report and Findings of the Safe School Initiative: Implications for the Prevention of School Attacks in the United States.* Washington, D.C., 2002. http://www.secretservice.gov/ntac/ssi_final_report.pdf.

University of Southern California. "USC Study Finds Faulty Wiring in Psychopaths." *Science Daily.* March 11, 2004. http://www.sciencedaily.com/releases/2004/03/040311 072248.htm.

Vail, Kathleen. "Words That Wound." *American School Board Journal* 37 (1999): 37–40.

Verdugo, Richard, Anamaria Vere, and the International Labour Organisation. *Workplace Violence in Service Sectors with Implications for the Education Sector: Issues, Solutions and Resources.* Working Paper no. 208. Geneva: International Labour Office, 2003.

Workplace Bullying Institute. "Results of the 2010 and 2007 WBI U.S. Workplace Bullying Survey." http://www.workplacebullying.org/wbiresearch/ 2010-wbi-national-survey.

World Health Organization. *World Report on Violence and Health.* Edited by Etienne G. Krug, Linda L. Dahlberg, James A. Mercy, Anthony B. Zwi, and Rafael Lozano. Geneva: World Health Organisation, 2002.

http://whqlibdoc.who.int/publications/2002/
9241545615_ eng.pdf.

Wynne, Richard, Nadia Clarkin, Tom Cox, and Amanda
          Griffiths. *Guidance on the Prevention of Violence at Work.*
          Luxembourg: European Commission, 1997.

Yang, Yaling, Adrian Raine, Katherine L. Narr, Patrick Colletti,
          and Arthur W. Toga. "Localization of Deformations
          within the Amygdala in Individuals with Psychopathy."
          Archives of General Psychiatry 66, no. 9 (2009): 986–94.

Zimmerman, Frederick J., Gwen M. Glew, Dimitri A. Christakis,
          and Wayne Katon. "Early Cognitive Stimulation,
          Emotional Support, and Television Watching as
          Predictors of Subsequent Bullying Among Grade-School
          Children." *Archives of Pediatrics and Adolescent Medicine* 159,
          no. 4 (2005): 384–8.

All links Checked and Accessed in September 2013.